Political Violence

Political Violence

by Ted Honderich

Cornell University Press

ITHACA, NEW YORK

First published 1976 by Cornell University Press.

International Standard Book Number 0–8014–1017–7
Library of Congress Catalog Card Number 76–4622

TYPESET IN INTERTYPE BASKERVILLE AND
PRINTED IN GREAT BRITAIN

Contents

To
Ruth and Bee

Introduction

These essays are what has come of my trying to inquire with an open mind into the morality of political violence, or really, political violence of the Left. To inquire, to try to get away from preconception and the like, this was my explicit intention, and indeed I have found my way to some propositions which are uncongenial to me. Still, I have done rather better at finding congenial ones. Perhaps this helps to show that to open one's mind is not necessarily to lose one's convictions.

It is sometimes said, still, in one way or another, that no question of moral justification arises about violence. It is not that the answer is obviously this, or obviously that, but that the question does not come up. There can be no question of right or wrong since, to speak plainly, violence is not really or finally a matter of the choice or decision of individuals. It is one more part of history's inevitable course. This doctrine of historical inevitability is attributed to Marx, of course, and the phrases used in its expression are well enough known. It has had, and will continue to have, some moral and political importance. I do not take it to be clear, or near to being settled as true, or indeed a doctrine which if true would make moral inquiry irrelevant. The latter supposition raises large and hard questions.

The members of a second party of amoralists about violence do allow that the question of morality arises but do not allow it importance. They regard it, in fact, as trivial. They are often enabled to do this by a misunderstanding, sometimes a misunderstanding of a wilful kind. That is, the question of the morality of violence is taken to be the question of how violence is regarded by the morally conventional, or by the morally naive, or by those who are blinded by class prejudice. To put this last possibility differently, the inquiry into the rightness or wrongness of violence is taken to be an inquiry directed by self-serving rotten moral principles. Such an inquiry is by definition worthless, and I trust, unremarkably, that mine is not of the kind. It would take a great deal of argument to establish that *any* inquiry, or any but a single chosen one, must of necessity be of the given low kind, or, to return to the other possibilities, a matter of mere conventionality or naiveté. Attempts have been made, in fact, to supply the argument for these or related conclusions. It would be unfair to suggest that they have always derived from what I have called misunderstanding.

There is a third and related group of amoralists. Its members do recognize that there is a question of the moral justification of violence, and they do not dismiss or diminish it in any of the ways just mentioned. That is not to say that they do not diminish it, however. There is said to be a second question of justification, but not of moral justification. This second question is the larger one and is given pride of place, to say the least. There is thought to be no doubt whatever that if violence is justified in this second way, that fact overwhelms its being morally justified or its being morally unjustified.

What is this other warrant that violence may have? In answer, the phrase 'the justification of history' may be heard, and such terms as 'social function' and 'historical meaning' and 'meaning for history'. We are to understand, perhaps, that present violence may be justified in the sense that at some future time it will come to be seen clearly that it did in fact make a necessary contribution to the achievement of some millenium. It may be either allowed or denied that we can somehow discern, in the present, that something is justified in this sense.

The confusion, it seems, is plain. What we are told, at bottom, is that violence may or may not make an essential contribution to a great good that is possible. The question of whether it will do so, therefore, far from being something separate, is a part of the question of moral justification. The question of whether violence will make a certain contribution to a millenium is not an independent and higher question, but something which must enter into the inquiry into the rightness or wrongness of violence. It enters in, of course, whether or not it can be answered now.

I mention these three related groups of amoralists, of disparagers of our question, not because I mean to try to deal in any sufficient way with any of their various propositions. My purpose is mainly to set them aside, some of them as friends misled, and hence to make clear at this early moment my own inclination. It is an orthodox one, that political violence does raise a question of moral justification, and that it raises that question above all.

The first essay, 'On Inequality and Violence, and Differences We Make Between Them', is unlike the others in not dealing with the question entirely by way of argument and reflection of a philosophical kind. That is, it is partly empirical. The facts which are brought to political philosophy, and I trust to its improvement, concern average lifetimes of certain groups and classes. For the rest, the particular subject of the first essay is certain of our first responses to the facts of inequality and the facts of violence, responses both in feeling and in doctrine. The essay is drawn from a lecture given to the Royal Institute of Philosophy.

Of the several pieces of reasoning by others which are examined in the second essay, and perhaps handled too roughly, one has to do first with the obligation to obey the law and to abstain from violence, and also with what is taken to be a conflicting and a higher demand. It is the work of Robert Paul Wolff. The other argument examined in the essay is founded on the idea of a social contract and issues in particular propositions about the obligation to obey the law and to abstain from violence. It also issues in two principles of justice for judging obligation, violence, and much else. It is the work of John Rawls. This second essay is drawn partly from a lecture given to the Oberlin Philosophy Colloquium and partly from a paper contributed to the journal, *Mind*.

'Democratic Violence', the third essay, concerns democracy and violence. It sets out an answer to the question of how violence stands to the practice and the rules of democracy, and, more importantly, an answer to the question of how violence stands to the ends or values which are proposed in the fundamental arguments for democracy. There is, as a result, analysis of a particular kind of violence, that kind named in the title of the essay. The essay comes from a lecture to the Third International Conference on the History of Ideas.

I am grateful for comments on particular arguments and claims to two of my colleagues, Jerry Cohen and Malcolm Budd, to Brian Barry, George Brennan, David Hamlyn, Alastair Hannay, Mihailo Markovic, Adam Schaff, and Allen Wood, and to graduate students who attended a term's seminar on Rawls's book at University College London.

I thank Helen Marshall for editorial admonitions, and Dinah Perry for exemplary work in the preparation of the manuscript.

By way of fuller bibliographical detail, the first essay is also published in *Nature and Conduct, Royal Institute of Philosophy Lectures* (London, 1975: Macmillan), edited by Richard Peters.

The Oberlin lecture, from which much of the second essay comes, is published as 'Appraisals of Political Violence', in *Issues in Law and Morality, Proceedings of the 1971 Oberlin Colloquium in Philosophy* (Cleveland and London, 1973: The Press of Case Western Reserve University), edited by Norman S. Care and Thomas Trelogan. *Issues in Law and Morality*, incidentally, also contains a reply to the lecture, by Edmund L. Pincoffs, and my rejoinder. The journal article from which the second essay also derives is 'The Use of the Basic Proposition of a Theory of Justice' (*Mind*, 1975).

A considerably shortened version of 'Democratic Violence' appears in *Violence and Aggression*, Proceedings of the Third International Conference of the International Society for the History of Ideas (New Brunswick, 1974: Rutgers University Press), edited by Philip P. Weiner and John Fisher. The essay also appears in the journal *Philosophy and Public Affairs* (Vol. 2, No. 2, 1973).

I am grateful to the various publishers for permissions.

I

On Inequality and Violence, and Differences We Make Between Them

Just about all political philosophy of the recommending kind is factless and presumptuous. That it has an honest intellectual use, which it does, and which of course is different from its use as a reassurance and the like, is only to be explained by the want of something better.

We can only agree that all of philosophy, in order to come within sight of its several ends, must have far less to do with empirical fact than those disciplines which has its discovery and explanation as their only end. However, in the political philosophy which implicitly or explicitly recommends action to us, or more likely inaction, premises of empirical fact necessarily have a larger importance than elsewhere in philosophy.

A reason for this larger importance is that recommendations of a quite specific nature are made. We are in fact urged to take a political side. Political philosophy of this kind is different even from moral philosophy of the traditional kind. There, one is urged only toward such indecisive parties as the Utilitarian and such indecisive commitments as to integrity. The Principle of Utility by itself, like a principle of integrity, does not decide particular questions in private morality for one. It is understood that to settle questions of conduct in marriage, say, one needs something in addition to general principles, which by themselves do not tell one what to do. The additional factual premises are not and could not easily be supplied, and so, very reasonably, recommendations of a specific nature are not made. One is not told what to do in marriage.

In political philosophy of the recommending kind, one is told what to do in politics. For such recommendations to rise to being *argued* recommendations, they clearly need to be preceded by premises about society, empirical premises of a pretty particular kind about conditions of life. Typically they are not. Nor does one have much confidence that what is said for our guidance was in fact derived, in private reflection off the page, from factual premises worth the name.

If political philosophy of the kind in question is as little empirical as the rest of philosophy, and has such need to be more so that it may with justice be called factless, it is therefore presumptuous in its conclusions. However, there is also presumption in it for an entirely different reason.

The issue of political violence, to come down to that, is typically handled in a mere essay or a mere chapter, which thing does nonetheless end with a conclusion on the principal question. We may be told that violence, leaving aside a few chosen revolutions now dignified or indeed hallowed by time, is savage iniquity. We may be given to understand, differently, perhaps in something that falls short of plain speech, that violence of the Left must reluctantly be welcomed. It may be allowed, as certainly it should be, that what has actually been set out in support of the chosen conclusion is no more than a *simulacrum* of the argument for it, or, certainly better, only *one part* of that argument. Still, we are offered the intimation that all of the real thing, the conclusive argument itself, exists somewhere else.

This political philosophy, then, begins without essential premises of fact, proceeds by way of intimation, and delivers conclusions to us nonetheless. Let us make a beginning at trying to put things right.

1. LIFETIMES

In the United States, on average, non-whites live for about 6.5 years less than whites.[1] About 25 *million* individuals now alive will have an average of about 6.5 years less of life than, on

[1] *Statistical Abstract of the United States: 1974* (Washington, 1975), Table 80, p. 58.

average, other members of their society. If there are no very fundamental economic and social changes in America, it is likely that the next 'generation', the non-whites who are alive 20 years from now, will have an improved life-expectancy but still one that is very considerably smaller than that of their white contemporaries. The rate of improvement in the past gives one basis among several for this guess about the future.[2] A more precise guess is that the non-whites alive 20 years from now, if fundamental economic and social changes do not come about, will have an average life-time about five years smaller than their white contemporaries.

The population of England and Wales has been divided into five of what are called social classes. They might also be called occupational groups, since they are in fact defined by the occupations of their members. They are labelled Professional, Intermediate, Skilled, Partly-skilled and Unskilled. On average, the life-expectancy of men in the fifth class, *at age 25*, is about 3.5 years less than the life-expectancy of their counterparts in the first social class.[3] The American figures for whites and non-whites, in contrast, have to do with life-expectancy at birth.

It is certain, although the figures are unavailable, that the average *whole* lifetime, the average life-expectancy at birth, of English and Welsh males in what can be called the unskilled class is considerably more than 3.5 years smaller than that of their counterparts in the professional class. There is evidence of several kinds for this.[4] Thus it is almost certain that well over a million individuals, compared with members of the professional class, will have shorter lifetimes by an average of about five years. One can guess that in 20 years' time, if fundamental social and economic

[2] In 1920 the gap between non-whites and whites was about 10 years, in 1930 about 13 years, in 1940 about 11 years, in 1950 about 8 years, in 1960 about 7 years, and in 1970 about 7 years. *Op. cit.*, Table 80, p. 58.
[3] Calculated from standard mortality indices in *The Registrar General's Decennial Supplement, England and Wales, 1961: Occupational Mortality Tables* (London, 1971).
[4] The difference in life expectancies between the fifth and the first social class is insignificant at age 65, 2.1 years at 55, 3 years at 35, and 3.3 years at 35, and 3.5 years at 25. (Calculated from standard mortality indices, *op. cit.*)

changes are not made in Britain, the unskilled class (or an ana-
logue) will be in an improved position but still have a life-expectancy very considerably smaller than that of a professional class.

Let us have before us, beside the truths and suppositions about
individual lifetimes in contemporary America and Britain, certain
uncontentious generalizations about all Western economically-
developed societies. We can proceed toward these by remembering
that non-whites in America and unskilled workers in Britain have
greatly less material wealth and income than other groups in their
societies.[5] There are, of course, some non-whites who are better
off than some whites, and some unskilled workers who are better
off than some members of some other occupational groups. On
the whole, nonetheless, non-whites in America and unskilled
workers and their families in Britain each are large parts of a
poorest group in each of the two societies. We have, then, a corre-
lation between an economic fact and a fact about lifetimes. It is
unsurprising. Indeed, the fact that the people in question come at
the bottom of scales of wealth and income is the principal part of
the complex cause of their shorter lives. This consideration, and
many related truths about groups in the other economically-
developed societies, give rise to the two generalizations I have in
mind, about all such societies.

The first one has to do with roughly the one-tenth of the present
population of each economically-developed society that has less
wealth and income than any other tenth in that society. The
generalization is that the worst-off tenth now living in each of the
developed societies will have considerably shorter lives than the
individuals in the best-off tenth. It is as good as certain that they
will live less long, on average, by five years or more. We must wait
for precision until the time, if ever it comes, when more statistical
work is done. The second generalization, as may be anticipated,
is that if there are not fundamental social and economic changes
in the societies in question, the situation will be better in 20 years
but not greatly better.

As in the case of what was said of America and Britain, the
numbers of people involved is of an obvious importance. There

[5] See, for example, A. B. Atkinson, *Wealth, Income and Inequality* (Harmondsworth, 1973).

are now, in all of the bottom tenths of the economically-developed societies, something like 65 *million* individuals.

To turn to a related subject-matter, the table below[6] gives a few specimen life-expectancies at birth for males and females, first for economically less-developed societies and then for developed societies. Males born in Gabon have an average lifetime of 25 years. Males born in Britain, taking all social classes together, have an average lifetime of 69, which approaches being three times as long. On *average*, males in Gabon die well before what is regarded as middle age in Britain.

LIFE EXPECTANCY AT BIRTH

	Gabon	Guinea	Nigeria	India	Colombia
Male	25	26	37	42	44
Female	45	28	37	41	46

	France	West Germany	America	England & Wales
Male	69	67	67	69
Female	76	73	75	75

The average lifetime of males and females taken together in all the less-developed societies, by one common definition of the latter, is about 42 years. The average lifetime of males and females together in developed countries, again with the latter defined in one common way, is about 71.[7] About *half the world's population*, then, have average lifetimes about 29 years shorter than another quarter of the world's population. It is not too much to say that what we have before us are *different kinds* of human lifetime.

The average figures for the two groups of societies, as the specimen figures indicate, hide still greater inequalities, those holding between particular societies. There is also the greater difference in lifetimes between the top tenth of population in all the developed countries and the bottom tenth of population in the

[6] Source: *United Nations Demographic Yearbook*, *1973* (New York, 1974), Table 18, p. 336. The figures in my table, like the figures in the source-table, have to do with different recent years.

[7] Simon Kuznets, 'The Gap: Concept, Measurement, Trends', p. 34, in *The Gap Between Rich and Poor Nations* (London, 1972) edited by Gustav Ranis.

less-developed countries. There are no figures available, to my knowledge, for the latter tenth. Given evidence of various kinds, it is certain that that bottom tenth in less-developed societies have average lifetimes very much more than 29 years shorter than the average lifetimes of the top tenth in developed societies. Their lives, on average, are in the neighbourhood of 40 years shorter. It is not too much to say, then, that the wealthiest in the wealthy countries have two lives for each single life of the poor in the poorest countries.

There is a likelihood that these inequalities in life-expectancy between developed and less-developed societies, and groups within them, will be smaller in 20 years. In the recent past, medical advances have improved life-expectancies in the less-developed societies, and it is likely that further advances will be made. Nonetheless, unless there is a transformation in the relations between the wealthy and the poor parts of the world, there will remain an immense difference in lifetimes 20 years from now.

The numbers of people involved in these propositions about the less-developed societies are of course very great. The population of the less-developed societies, as defined, about half of the world's population, includes about *1,700 million people*. The bottom tenth then includes about *170 million people*.

There arises the question of the possibility of any real change, either in the inequalities of lifetime within developed societies or in the inequalities of lifetime between developed and less-developed societies. Some will be inclined to suppose that whatever morality may say or not say, we do not have the relevant capability. Thus there is misconception in talk of large changes in lifetimes that might follow on fundamental social and economic changes. It may be objected, in effect, that it is already inevitable that the next generation of the groups in question will have a life-expectancy much like that of the present generation of the same groups.

This is mistaken, certainly or probably. Given the wealth and efficiency of the developed societies, proved in many different ways, it is clear enough that we could change very radically the life-expectancy of the groups in question. One needs to reflect, in part, on the magnitude of just such changes in the past. To consider the inequalities *within* developed societies, the following table gives the change in life-expectancy of American whites, at birth, over a period of 40 years.[8]

1920	54.9
1940	64.2
1960	70.6

One fact of relevance, then is that in each of two 20-year periods in the recent past, the life-expectancy of American whites was improved to a considerably greater extent than would be required in the coming 20 years if American blacks were to come up to the level of American whites.

It is to be admitted, certainly, that the case is not clear with respect to the possibility of change in the lifetime-inequalities between developed and less-developed societies. Nonetheless, it is beyond question that the inequalities could be dramatically reduced. The lifetime-inequalities are consequences of economic inequalities. It is my own view that no amount of economic theory can put in doubt the truth that the present economic inequalities are open to change, change which would not be damaging to present economic totals and which would dramatically reduce lifetime-inequalities.

It is worth remarking in this connection, to those who are struck by how very little *has* been achieved, that not much more than nothing has been attempted. In 1964 a number of the economically-developed countries pledged to 'contribute' a percentage of their future gross national products to the less-developed countries. This 'contribution' was to include loans and private investment. The figure agreed upon was 1%. Since that time, a number of the countries in question have failed to reach this percentage. None has exceeded it by much. The pledged total of 1% of the gross national products of the developed countries in question has not been met in any year.[9] This is not the *kind* of thing to be kept in mind in considering the question of capability. A better thing is the 'war efforts' of the past.

[8] Source: *Statistical Abstract of the United States, 1974*, Table 80, p. 58.

[9] Robert McNamara, *Address to the Board of Governors* of the International Bank for Reconstruction and Development (1970), p. 8.

B

All of these generalizations about lifetimes have *all* of their importance in the fact that they have to do with *individual human experience*. It is a banal truth that typically we escape this proposition, or give it the attention of a moment. It is necessary to come closer to the reality of experience. We may do so through one woman's recorded recollection of her daughter.

She was doing fine, real fine. I thought she was going to be fine, too. I did. There wasn't a thing wrong with her, and suddenly she was in real trouble, bad trouble, yes sir, she was. She started coughing, like her throat was hurting, and I thought she must be catching a cold or something. I thought I'd better go get her some water, but it wasn't easy, because there were the other kids, and it's far away to go. So I sent my husband when he came home, and I tried to hold her, and I sang and sang, and it helped. But she got real hot, and she was sleepy all right, but I knew it wasn't good, no sir. I'd rather hear her cry, that's what I kept saying. My boy, he knew it too. He said, 'Ma, she's real quiet, isn't she?' Then I started praying, and I thought maybe it'll go the way it came, real fast, and by morning there won't be anything but Rachel feeling a little tired, that's all. We got the water to her, and I tried to get her to take something, a little cereal, like she was doing all along. I didn't have any more milk—maybe that's how it started. And I had a can of tomato juice, that we had in case of real trouble, and I opened it and tried to get it down her. But she'd throw it all back at me, and I gave up, to tell the truth. I figured it was best to let her rest, and then she could fight back with all the strength she had, and as I said, maybe by the morning she'd be the winner, and then I could go get a bottle of milk from my boss man and we could really care for her real good, until she'd be back to her self again. But it got worse, I guess, and by morning she was so bad there was nothing she'd take, and hot all over, she was hot all over. And then she went, all of a sudden. There was no more breathing, and it must have been around noon by the light.[10]

[10] Robert Coles, *Still Hungry in America* (Cleveland, 1969), pp. 27–8.

To my mind, no breath of apology is owed to those who may say that they do not expect to find emotional matter within serious reflection. On the contrary, one must feel remiss for offering so small a reminder of human experience, or feel a despondency in the realization that so little will be tolerated.

2. VIOLENCE

The facts of violence are not so much in need of being brought forward. It is a part of what I shall discuss in this essay that we have an immediate and a sharp awareness of them. Nonetheless, should anyone persist in regarding the effects of violence as no more than calculable expenses to be paid for the march of history, it will be as well to assert what should need no asserting, that here too we find facts of human experience. Bombs injure, maim, and kill. They end or devastate the lives of their first victims and they bring agony or ruin to the lives of their second victims, those who suffer through others being injured, maimed, or killed. The effects of explosions are not only those effects which we find detailed in our newspapers. A man who is blinded or a girl who loses a hand lives on, and, for everyone who is killed, there are others who continue to be affected.

If these are the things of importance about political violence, there is need for a general definition. Political violence, roughly defined, is *a considerable or destroying use of force against persons or things, a use of force prohibited by law, directed to a change in the policies, personnel or system of government, and hence also directed to changes in the existence of individuals in the society and perhaps other societies.* There are other definitions of political violence, certainly, including definitions thought to be more enlightened or virtuous, and we shall return to the matter.[11]

It will be as well to have in mind some extent or magnitude of political violence. What I shall have in mind in what follows is roughly the level of violence with which we have become familiar in Britain, America and elsewhere in the world during the past

[11] See below, Essay 2, Part 1, and Essay 3, Part 2. See also Jerome A. Shaffer (ed), *Violence* (New York, 1971), which contains several essays on the definition of violence.

decade. To put the matter differently, if no more precisely, I shall have in mind campaigns of violence but not violence at the level of civil war. Nor, of course, shall we be concerned with war between nations, which does not fall under the definition of political violence.

Finally, by way of preliminaries, it may be worth pointing out that more will be in question than exactly the violence which has been most common during the past decade. There can be violence directed to other ends than those with which we are most familiar. We shall be concerned with political violence generally, which is to say both actual and possible violence.

3. FACTS AND REASONINGS

There are the facts of violence, then, and there are what we may call, if we persist in the use of an anodyne label, the facts of inequality. The latter, of which we have considered only one particular set, claim our attention not only because they consist in *inequalities*: situations such that one group of people has *less* of something than another. It is not merely that some people have less, but that they have *so little*, judged in an absolute rather than a comparative way. They are in conditions of deprivation or distress or worse. The circumstance is not an unreal one which can be imagined, where inequality does not matter much because the worst-off are nonetheless splendidly-off. Our real circumstance is one in which the facts of inequality include, and might alternatively and summarily be described as, the facts of deprivation, distress and suffering. Yet again they might with at least some reason be called the facts of oppression.

My intentions in this essay, which have to do with these facts and with the facts of violence, are two in number. One of them, with whatever success, has already been realized. It is to make a contribution, no more than a small one, and however 'unphilosophical', to a realization of the facts of inequality. Any such realization, of course, must bear on violence as well. The particular set of facts noticed, those about inequality in quantity of life, have a natural priority. *Time alive* is not all that matters, but it matters very much indeed. Still, I do not mean to give this set of inequalities a greater importance, or for that matter a lesser importance, than others. The other facts of inequality may be separated into two further sets. There are those many inequalities which have to do with economic and social life. The list begins with inequalities in food, shelter and health. The extent of such inequalities is only barely indicated by the known immense disparities in wealth and income. The third set of inequalities are political in kind, and have to do with certain freedoms and the lack of them. It is here that one finds demands for equality in national self-determination, and demands for equality between peoples in certain large possessions, notably lands to which there are historical rights.

It cannot be that rationality allows us to avoid informing ourselves of these things which are more or less directly relevant to violence. No more is meant than said: that we are obliged in rationality *to inform ourselves.* As I have already implied, a part of this is a decent approach to human experience in its detail. What is needed first is knowledge, knowledge of particulars, which is to be distinguished from responses of feeling to the facts of inequality, and from judgements about them. No one should overlook, for example, that shorter lifetimes are in clear ways within the anticipation of very many of those who have them and also within the experience of others. With respect to the latter point, there is the fact that if she had lived longer, the death of the daughter would not ever have been within the experience of the mother.

If we were better informed of the facts of inequality, we could with propriety pass on to further things. What is customarily done, as I have remarked, is to press on improperly, to conclusions. What we shall do here, somewhat less improperly, is to move forward slowly. We shall not come to a conclusion about the rightness, the permissibility, the wrongfulness or the heinousness of political violence. The matters we shall consider, like the facts of inequality and violence, have a natural place near the beginning of an orderly inquiry.

There is a certain welter of propositions, arguments, theories and doctrines which comes in between the factual premises about inequality and violence and any final conclusions about the morality of violence. I mean, in saying that these things come in, that they must be considered. All of them are reasons or reasonings, or else they can be improved into reasons or reasonings. All of them, obviously, must be made decently clear and explicit before their value is judged. In the end, of course, since they point in different directions, some of them must be rejected, or regarded as of lesser weight.

Here are some examples, all of one kind. We may believe that some governments, perhaps democratic ones, have a rightful authority over the members of the societies in question, and hence that the members have an obligation of obedience. We may believe that all members of a society, simply by living in it, acquire an obligation to keep some or all of its laws. We may have some idealized conception of the society of justice, and suppose that our actual society is within sight of realizing this conception. Very differently, we may have some ordered set of fundamental moral principles, or a belief as to the best or the only acceptable way of drawing moral conclusions, perhaps a way that is thought to guarantee fairness.[12] Differently, we may be committed to a number of propositions, perhaps got by historical inquiry, about the probability that violence will secure or give rise to social change. Differently again, we may suppose that some political violence has important affinities with the practice of democracy.

Whatever their final value, such reasons and reasonings are certainly of relevance to any verdict on violence. I shall consider some of them, including the last one, in the second and third essays of this book. Still, these are examples of reasons and reasonings of a kind correctly described as being at a certain distance from the facts, the facts of inequality and of violence. There are things which are closer to the facts and which may be considerably more persuasive for many people, whether or not they should be such. Some of these latter things, indeed, may determine the weight given to the more distant reasons and reasonings. They

[12] I have in mind such a procedure as the one made clear by R. M. Hare, *Freedom and Reason* (Oxford, 1963). For an economical and acute account of reasonings found in the history of political theory, see Leslie J. Macfarlane, *Political Disobedience* (London, 1971). Hannah Arendt, in 'On Violence', an essay in *Crises of the Republic* (Harmondsworth, 1973), discusses some of them enlighteningly.

often have the character of unreflective responses and assumptions, but, as I have said, they can be other than that. My second intention in this essay is to look at four of them, perhaps the four which are most important. They have to do with feelings about inequality and violence, the existence of moral prohibitions on certain kinds of action, the supposed irrationality of violence, and the possibility of having satisfactory principles of equality.

4. FEELINGS

If we were to assemble the facts of inequality before ourselves as best we could, as we have not done, what would be our untutored feelings about them? Among the facts would be those at which we have looked. (i) Within economically developed societies a bottom tenth of individuals, about 65 million people, have lives at least five years shorter on average than other members of their societies. (ii) About half the world's population, that of the less-developed societies, have average lifetimes about 29 years shorter than another quarter of the world's population. (iii) One can say with reason that the worst-off in the less developed countries, about 170 million people, have *one* life for the *two* lives of the best-off in the developed countries. Among the facts of inequality before us, as well, would be those of socio-economic and political kinds. Also, for all these general facts, there would be particulars, particulars of human experience.

We are, we may suppose, people who are moved to some decent degree by the situations of others and have only an ordinary amount of prejudice. We are not *possessed* by ideology or doctrine. We may, as people do, incline to certain social and economic beliefs, but these are not so much a part of us that we have no independent attitude to the facts of inequality.

What would be our untutored feelings about them? The question could do with sharper expression, but let us take it as we have it. Our feelings in the imagined state of knowledge would be considerably different from our ordinary responses now, in our actual state of ignorance. As I have already implied, we feel less than we might about the facts of inequality, much less, simply because we are ignorant of them. That, however, is not my

present concern, which may be approached by noticing that our
untutored feelings would have a certain *character*. Many of us,
faced with the facts of inequality, would be appalled, dismayed,
saddened, affected, sympathetic, wearied, bitter or resentful. The
character of these feelings is one of passivity or quietness.

Suppose that on another occasion we have assembled before
us the facts of violence. Suppose we have before us killing, wounding, such destruction of property as touches closely on the lives of
individuals, and also the consequences of these several things. The
difference between what we are imagining and what is the case,
between our having full knowledge and our having the knowledge we actually have, is far less here than with the inequalities.

Many of all of us would feel horror, shock, repugnance, dis-
gust, rage or vengefulness. The terms 'atrocity' and 'savagery'
would very likely have a place in the expression of these emotions.
To come to the principal point, these emotions do not have about
them the passivity or quietness of the emotions called up by the
facts of inequality. They have a different character.

This difference is a fact about the feelings which we would
have, given a fuller knowledge of inequality and violence, but
obviously there is a related fact about the feelings we actually
do have, with the knowledge we actually do have. It has seemed
to me right to come to the matter by way of insistence that we be
more responsible about informing ourselves. Certainly it is the
difference in *informed* feelings, as they might be called, which is
most important. In what follows, nonetheless, we shall almost
inevitably have in mind our feelings as they are, and this will
not be disastrous. It will certainly not be to the advantage of my
argument, but rather the reverse.

Feelings about inequality and violence are obviously of great
effect on final moral views about violence. Furthermore, it is
certainly possible to regard the responses as *reasons*, or to derive
reasons from them. That is, it can be argued that we ought to be
directed in our judgements by such differences in feeling, that
such differences are right determinants of judgement.

The general ideas that we are guided by feeling in morality,
and that we ought to be, are somehow true. That is, some understanding of these ideas makes them beyond denial. Obviously,
both matters are complex ones. Let us look a bit at the second

one, to the effect that we ought to be guided by differences in feeling.

It is clear enough that we must pay attention to what can be called the circumstance of feeling. We must look to the question of how it is that we come to feel as we do. Few people will say, except in heat, or with personal excuse, that we should not inquire into this. Very nearly all recent moral philosophy, in one way or another, gives explicit adherence to a general proposition of this kind about feeling, despite the fact that this philosophy has not got down to hard cases and hard details. What I should like to consider is whether our circumstance is such that we can give an unquestioned importance to our feelings about inequality and violence. There are a number of quite plain propositions which are of relevance. Things go unnoticed which are there for the eye to see.

One notable difference between any consideration of the two orders of fact is that the *agents* of violence are inevitably in the foreground and the agents of inequality are not immediately to be seen. The man who sets a bomb or shoots another man is precisely within our focus. Not so with agents of inequality. We may of course set out to find them. We may attempt some distinction of the kind that has informed whole traditions of reflection and politics, and issued in works with such titles as 'Their Morals and Ours'.[13]

If we attempt this, we may have some tolerable success. We shall certainly find a class of people who may be said to accede to the system of inequalities, and who could contribute to change. It does not stand in the way of this enterprise that their motivations and personalities are not greatly different from those of the victims of inequality. They do not contribute to change and, unlike almost all of the victims of inequality, they could do so. Their simplest contribution would be part of their wealth.

At least three relevant things are true of this class of agents of inequality. One is that very nearly all of us are members of the class. A second is that the class is immense and hence, so to speak, anonymous. Its members are not some few identified individuals. The third is that the relation of these agents to the facts of

[13] By Leon Trotsky.

inequality is quite unlike the relation of the agents of violence to the facts of that order. No one with his own hands sets a fuse which secures an immense loss of living time for American blacks or a part of the British population. Much of the latter difference, which I shall not pause to detail, remains if we narrow down our conception of the agents of inequality to individuals who actively obstruct change or, differently, individuals who by their own actions do make for the distress of identifiable victims of inequality.

Our feeling about violence, then, has very much to do with its agents, while our feeling about inequality has less or indeed little to do with its agents. The latter is true because the agents of inequality are pretty well out of sight or, if they are in sight, they are ourselves, they are many and impersonal, and they are distant from their work. The character of our feeling about violence, against the character of our feeling about inequality, is in significant part explained by the matter of agents.

However, to move toward the principal point, there is reason for saying that our feelings about inequality and violence are principally relevant insofar as they are feelings about victims rather than agents. That, although we shall in a way come back to the question, will be agreed by almost all who consider inequality and violence, no matter to what conclusion they are inclined. What matters is suffering, distress and deprivation, and not, by itself, what may be regarded as an agent's callous deliberateness in intention. It is impossible to agree with Kant that a good will, or a bad will, matters far more than its effects on others, that a good will is the only unqualifiedly good thing and a bad will, presumably, the only unqualifiedly bad thing. If we could subtract all bad and terrible intentions *or* all suffering from the world, we would rightly not be in doubt for a moment about which to do. We thus have a consideration which must lead us in some degree to discount the vehemence, indeed the violence, of our feeling about violence. If that vehemence were more the product of an awareness of victims, and less the product of an awareness of agents, the circumstance would be importantly different.

There is a complication with which we shall be faced. There are those who will urge upon us a persistent Utilitarianism, or one or another doctrine akin to it. They will object that if it is agreed that our concern must principally be with victims, it must also be agreed as a consequence that we must concern ourselves with agents, conceived just as causers of distress, makers of victims. That is, we must look upon agents of violence as we look upon ordinary non-political lawbreakers if we subscribe to the deterrence theory of punishment. Like an ordinary offender, a man who sets a bomb is a man who is likely to act in the same way again and also a man who encourages others to do likewise.

It may thus be suggested, by way of a ramshackle argument, that we should in no way discount our feeling about violence on the ground that it is to some significant degree called up by agents. The argument, in essence, will be that any discounting of feeling leads to inhibition of it, that inhibition will have an effect on what is done to agents, and that if less is done there will be more victims.

Of course, the same sort of premise may also be taken to lead in another direction, toward doubt about the validity of our passive or quiet response to the facts of inequality. That is, the premise may be thought also to contribute to the conclusion that we should have stronger feelings about the agents of inequality, or compensate in our reflection for the weakness of our feelings. I shall not examine either this retort or the Utilitarian argument about violence. All I wish to notice is that we are not in fact persistently Utilitarian, or anything like it. Our responses to the agents of violence, perhaps, are in part 'useful' responses to causes of distress or, in the relevant sense, makers of victims. However, our responses are very much more than that. They are accusatory or vengeful. The machine that maims a worker and the man who maims another man are naturally regarded by us in quite different ways. In the latter case, there is the fact of our beliefs and attitudes having to do with responsibility and culpability of persons. Hence, even should we be inclined to give some attention to the Utilitarian argument about feeling, it would remain the case that our feeling about the facts of violence has much to do with agents regarded as other than past and perhaps future causes of distress.

In sum, the different characters of our feelings about violence and inequality has in part to do with our awareness of some agents and our want of awareness of others. To the extent that the resulting feelings are not related to the matter of prevention, they are not of the first importance. What is of the first importance is feeling about victims. We have, then, a reason for questioning a large reliance on the contrast in our feelings about violence and inequality.

A second plain proposition about our different responses to inequality and violence has to do with the *familiarity* of inequality, which is everywhere, and the *unfamiliarity* of violence. The magnitude of inequalities, and the absolute as against the comparative condition of those who are worst-off, are not things of which we have much grasp. Still, if we were to assemble the facts of inequality, we would not then have a grasp of something with which we had had no previous familiarity. As for violence not being within the experience of most of us, that is no doubt a generality pertaining only to most times and most places. As such, it stands high among useful generalizations in political philosophy.

It is to be remarked, then, that the quiet feelings evoked by inequality are in part to be explained by the relative familiarity of the subject-matter. The feelings evoked by violence are in part to be explained by the relative unfamiliarity of violence. There is support for this in the truism that there is a deadening or quieting of feeling in certain circumstances, usually in war, when violence becomes familiar.

The suggestion that must emerge here is that the moral relevance of feelings is the less if they owe something, perhaps a good deal, to the familiarity or unfamiliarity of their objects. It surely cannot be that the 'natural' death of a child or the murder of a man has a significantly different value in virtue of there being many or few such deaths, many or few murders. One may think of ways in which the proposition might be qualified, but the qualifications are slight ones, of a secondary importance. Thus our circumstance in responding to inequality and violence is for a second reason one in which our first feelings are not to be accorded an unquestioned deference.

A third thing to be considered has to do with the common perception of inequality as *entrenched*. Violence is rightly seen differently. Setting a bomb is a human action which like other human actions might not have been performed. The man could have done otherwise. That, however the belief is to be analysed, is our belief. The action is something, too, which quickly raises in the mind the possibility of prevention by others. The inequalities, by contrast, and for good reason, do not have the perceived character of things that easily might not have been, or things that we can briskly set about altering.

The point again is that if our feelings about human experience are in part given their character by a factor external to that experience, such a fact must be paid attention. If the quiet of our feelings about inequality is in part owed to a perception of inequality as settled and resistant, this is a fact to be paid attention. The terribleness of human experience, the terribleness of having a child whose lifetime is five years, remains just that, whatever may be true about persistence and change. If the inequalities were not merely entrenched, but in fact necessary and inevitable, which is different, the situation would be otherwise. That they are in fact necessary and inevitable is a simple error corrected by some reflection on history.

It is to be admitted, certainly, that it would be irrational to come to a verdict about political violence without paying careful attention to the probability of its actually achieving ends of social change. That is something of which I shall have more to say. However, it is one thing to take the matter into account, in full consciousness and in the right place, and another thing not to notice its effect on our feelings about the human experience of inequality.

Fourthly, it is at least arguable that our feelings about inequalities and about violence are influenced by the correct perception of the inequalities as constituting a state of *order*, and violence as constituting a circumstance of *disorder*. Inequality is a product of law, of diverse settled institutions, of custom and indeed of assent. The vast majority of those who are worst-off do not resist, because they cannot. Violence is otherwise. A man shot by a political assassin is one of two figures in a circumstance of a wholly different character, a circumstance of anarchy. No restraint is put on one's feeling about his death by a recognition of it as ordained.

To repeat, if our concern is rightly our feelings *about the experience of others*, it is important to be sure that we take into account precisely these feelings. The present point, then, is that the pain and distress of others should not come upon one, in the first instance, as items of order or of disorder. It may be that they should be so considered, at some later point in reflection. They should not be regarded in this way in the first instance if a primary matter is not to be confused. If, therefore, pain and distress *do* in fact have an effect upon us which is partly a consequence of something that is external to them, we must recognize this fact.

A fifth consideration has to do with the difference, not necessarily a reasonable difference, in our response to being attacked or wounded on the one hand, and, on the other, being distressed or made to suffer for much longer periods but not as a consequence of being attacked, wounded or the like. Before one argues too quickly from the primitive impulse to choose, say, lasting hunger rather than an injury, it is useful to consider what one would choose for another person, perhaps a person about whom one cares. It is safe to observe that first impulses are not certain to be last judgements. A sixth consideration has to do with the indiscriminateness or the undirectedness of much political violence. One thing to be remarked here is that the particular victims of inequality are not carefully chosen either. However, I shall leave undiscussed these considerations, the fifth and the sixth, and finish here with something else.

Engels, in *Anti-Duhring*, characterizes all of morality as class morality.[14] It is, in his view, an instrument of the ruling class or an instrument of an oppressed but rising class. A somewhat less *simpliste* view is advanced by Marx and Engels in the *German Ideology*.[15] Bentham and Mill also have views which touch on the general matter.[16] One proposition in this area, one which does not presuppose a ruling class's *devising* of morality, is that some moral feeling has some of its genesis in a self-identification which is general among the members of ascendant classes.

The relative quietness of our feelings about inequality, and the violence of our feelings about violence, are related to our own

---

[14] *Herr Eugen Duhring's Revolution in Science (Anti-Duhring)*, trans. E. Burns (New York), p. 109.

[15] Marx-Engels, *The German Ideology*, ed. R. Pascal (London, 1939).

[16] Bentham, *The Handbook of Fallacies*, p. 207. Mill, *On Liberty*, p. 70 (Everyman edition).

places in the world. You who are reading this essay, in all likelihood, are a beneficiary of the system of inequality and, perhaps
more important, have no human connection with the victims of
that system. By contrast, in many ordinary situations of life, you
discount the feelings and doubt the judgements of individuals
who are in certain positions of benefit and relationship analogous
to your own.

It is remarkable that such suggestions of self-deception or at
any rate self-concern are dismissed by those who are familiar with
a society some of whose fundamental institutions are constructed
so as to defeat such things as self-deceiving responses to groups
other than one's own. It will be remarkable, too, if such suggestions of self-deception and the like continue to be dismissed by
philosophers. No recent work of moral philosophy lacks a device
against self-deceiving self-interest in its recommended system of
reflection. In some cases, the device is most of the system.

Some may regard some or all of the foregoing seven reflections
on inequality and on violence as ill-judged or tasteless. This may
have to with a failure to recognize that there are *two* orders of
fact, each of them compelling, each of them terrible. Not to
recognize this is to fail in feeling and judgement. Again, there
is an inclination to suppose the the question of political violence,
like any serious moral question, is one for ourselves as *moral
judges*. That is, it is a question for the moral consciousness or the
moral self, or perhaps the conscience. It is not one of which we can
rightly treat by bringing in empirical psychology, propositions
about the causes of feeling. This inclination, to my mind, is not
one to be encouraged. The moral consciousness, somehow insu-
lated from our attitudes and situations, is a fiction, and not a good
one.

5. PROHIBITIONS

There are moral philosophers and the like who say, whether or
not they would always do as they say, that there are certain kinds
of act which are absolutely prohibited. These are acts about
which there can never be a moral question, acts which must never
be done whatever the circumstances. Those who express this

view, which is connected with religious tradition, do not have in mind such 'truisms' as this, that an act is prohibited if *all* that is known of it is that it would cause suffering. They have in mind certain familiar acts, identified in quite different ways. One kind may be the killing of another person, an innocent person.

It is unlikely that many people would hesitate if they were faced with a straight and clear choice between killing a man on the one hand, and, on the other hand, inaction of which they *believed with certainty* that it would give rise to catastrophic consequences, perhaps many deaths. If, as is far from being the case, they were faced with a choice between an act of killing and, on the other hand, inaction taken to involve the *near-certainty* of catastrophic consequences, many would choose the killing and would defend their choice. Doctrines about absolute moral prohibitions have lost any pervasiveness they may once have had.

Nonetheless, there is no doubt that there exists an inclination or perhaps something more than that, a conviction, against certain acts and those who perform them. It is not the claim that there is an *absolute* prohibition, but it is somewhere in the direction of that conclusion. What is in question here, as before, is the idea that an act of killing, say, is somehow wrong in itself, and not that it is wrong because in fact it will not be effective in securing an end, say social or economic change. There is thought to be a kind of moral constraint upon us which does not have anything to do with the consequences of action or inaction. It is a constraint which has to do with acts in themselves, and one which sometimes may rightly be effective in preventing individuals from doing what would have the best consequences.

This is the second of the responses to inequality and political violence which I wish to consider in this essay. It may be an unconsidered reaction to acts of violence and to those who perform them, either when lives are taken or endangered, or in other cases as well. Alternatively, it may be more reflective. In both forms, rightly or wrongly, it has been persuasive with many people.

The kind of inclination or conviction in question may of course arise in cases that do not have to do with political violence. Bernard Williams, in *Utilitarianism, For and Against*, considers the example of a chemist, without a job and hence with his family in difficulty, who is offered work in a laboratory whose research is into chemical and biological warfare.[17] He, unlike his wife, is particularly opposed to such warfare and to the research. However, he understands that if he refuses the job, the research will proceed anyway. More important, he knows that if he refuses the job, it will go to a particular man who is likely to push along the research with greater zeal than he himself would. The chemist nonetheless refuses the job. It is recommended to us that he has done the right thing. The acute argument for this recommendation has to do with two things, integrity and responsibility.

In refusing the job, we are to understand, the chemist's action flowed from deep attitudes which are fundamental to the person he is. He has not acted as a consequence of the attitudes or actions of another, in such a way as to alienate himself from his own actions, and hence in such a way as to diminish or destroy his own integrity, his integrity in the most literal sense. He would have diminished or destroyed his integrity if he had taken the job, as a consequence of the fact that the other chemist would be more diligent in the research. He would, in that case, have been acting as a consequence of the attitudes and actions of the other man.[18]

To pass on to responsibility, the chemist does take the view, understandably enough, that one of the two possible states of affairs would be *better* than the other. The better one, of course, is the one in which he himself does take the job and hence the research goes forward more slowly than it would in the hands of the other man. However, the chemist also takes it that it is not his business to engage in this state of affairs. It is not *his* business to prepare, however less efficiently than someone else might, for chemical and biological warfare. There is a great difference for him between this possible state of affairs and the worse one. Although he himself is involved in the coming-about of the worse state of affairs, *the other chemist does the job* and hence 'a vital link in the production of the eventual outcome is provided by *someone else's* doing something.'[19]

It is allowed that in refusing to take the job the first chemist is responsible, in some sense of the word, for the fact that the

[17] J. J. C. Smart and Bernard Williams, *Utilitarianism: For and Against* (London, 1973), pp. 97–8.
[18] *Op. cit.*, pp. 116–17, pp. 103–4.
[19] *Op. cit.*, p. 94.

C

research will go forward more quickly than it might. However, this will only come about through the other man's actions. The first chemist cannot be said to *make* this happen, and, it is suggested, he rightly does not accept a full responsibility for the outcome.

In all of this we do have an illumination of the common inclination against certain acts. Certainly there is a great deal of difference between the case of the chemist and the case of a man who contemplates an act of political violence. Nonetheless, any considerations which apply to the chemist also apply to the other man. We may have the inclination that he should be such a man as the chemist. He should be of a certain integrity, and he should maintain that integrity by not engaging in violence, even though he believes that the consequences of his engaging in violence will be, or are likely to be, better than the consequences of his not doing so.

The inclination needs examination, and for several reasons it will be best to proceed by way of the given example of the chemist. There is one preliminary. The inclination is in conflict with several general attitudes to the effect that we ought always to act in such a way as to produce the best or the least bad state of affairs. One such general attitude is that we ought always to act in such a way as to produce *the least total of distress*. The case of the chemist is indeed offered against this proposition, which is the Principle of Utility in one formulation. However, the inclination also comes into play against the attitude, to speak very quickly indeed, that we should always act in such a way as to produce *that state of affairs which most avoids inequality and distress*.

This attitude, which has informed some of my earlier remarks, and of which I shall say more, is the fundamental part of the most common of reflective moralities. It, like Utilitarianism, is 'consequentialist'. It takes into account only what may be called the consequences of action, although more consequences than are considered in Utilitarianism. It conflicts with the inclination having to do with integrity which has been mentioned. In order to be consistent, and I think more relevant, let us have in mind this particular consequentialist attitude. Let us imagine what is certainly reasonable, that the chemist in refusing the job does something which makes *inequality and distress* more likely. His action conflicts with the particular consequentialist principle to the effect that we should pursue the states of affairs which include, or are likely to produce, the least inequality and distress.

The main difficulty about the case, it seems to me, is that of actually finding what consideration or principle it is which is supposed to lead us to agree that the chemist's act in refusing the job is right. That consideration or principle is not actually supplied to us. Let us see what, if anything, can be found.

We are told that the chemist preserves his integrity in refusing the job. This may amount to different things. The first of them, which must be got out of the way, is the *matter of fact* that the chemist, in refusing the job, is acting in accordance with deep attitudes of his own. His action is in no sense in conflict with these attitudes, whatever they are. Hence we say, if obscurely, that there exists a unity or a whole. *He* remains whole. Integrity, in a literal sense, is maintained. In this, however, we have no consideration whatever that might lead us to agree that refusing the job is the right thing to do. It seems obvious enough that there is no connection whatever between the described integrity and right acts. An act of integrity in this sense, given certain imaginable deep attitudes on the part of an agent, will be an act of absolute immorality. Nothing follows about the rightness or wrongness of the act from the fact alone that it is in line with an agent's deep attitudes, which presumably may be of any kind.

To say the chemist preserves his integrity by refusing the job, then, is necessarily to do something other than state a morally irrelevant and somewhat obscure matter of fact. It is to approve of him, to commend him. It may be to approve of him or to commend him because, as we may say, he is *true to himself*. The chemist perseveres in certain deep attitudes. It is obviously important what they are. Here there is some obscurity, but it may be that the attitudes are to the effect that *he himself, with his own hands, should not carry forward research into chemical and biological war*. He persists in this attitude even when he sees that it issues in making chemical and biological war more likely. The chemist, then, is true to himself.

There are several related things to be said about this second speculation as to the matter of integrity. One is that there seems to be very little relevant connection between a man being commendable in the given way and his act being right. A man, it seems, can be commendable for the reason that he is true to himself no matter what act he performs, so long as he himself is morally committed to it. All that is required is that he sticks to his moral convictions, whatever they are. An appallingly wrong act, perhaps one of pointless torture, does not move a bit in the direction of being right when we learn that the torturer is being true to himself. What changes, perhaps, is our view of him.

There is the possibility of a confusion at this point. Surely, someone may object, we can support a man in his act, to which he is committed, for the reason that things work out better in the end if people are true to themselves. More importantly, we may sometimes even support a man if *we* think his act is somehow wrong. Several questions are raised by this objection, but it would be confusion to think that it is an effective one. The objector asserts the value of our being true to ourselves in order to object to consequentialism. However, the objection itself derives from consequentialism. In part it is that the effects, perhaps in terms of distress and inequality, will be better if people are true to themselves. However, what we are trying to find in the case of the chemist is a consideration or a reason of a non-consequentialist kind, a consideration or a reason for doing what is likely *not* to have the best effects.

The second thing to be said about commending the chemist is to be distinguished from the point that his act may be wrong even if he is true to some commitment. It is that if we are even to commend *him*, and, more important, if there is to be so much as a *question* of commending him, we must believe that he does really have something that is distinguishable as a *moral* attitude or a *moral* commitment. We cannot commend a man for integrity on the ground that he is, so to speak, true to his selfishness. An absolutely unswerving record of acting in one's own interests does not establish integrity.

What then is the chemist's moral attitude or commitment? As we have noticed already, he does have *an* attitude: he is opposed to carrying forward research into chemical and biological warfare with his own hands, even though the only alternative is *more effective* research by someone else. Is that a moral commitment? It will occur to everyone that the chemist, in leaving the job to the man who will do more effective research, is simply engaged in keeping his own hands clean. Better that someone else should make a larger contribution to a terrible eventuality than that he should make a smaller one. Better that chemical and biological war should be slightly *more* likely than that he himself should have his hands in it. The chemist may be said to be engaged, if one puts the point in Williams' own way, which might be thought to endanger it by overstatement, in 'self-indulgent squeamishness'.[20]

Williams replies that the point is not independent of the assertion of a consequentialist morality. If the point were addressed to the chemist, it would necessarily be no more than an invitation to reconsider his decision, and in particular to reconsider it from a consequentialist point of view. The criticism would not consist in an independent argument, which is what is required, but simply a reiteration of the opposed morality.

This reply seems to me partly right and importantly wrong. The criticism is in a certain sense not an argument, but it need not be merely an invitation to reconsider either. It may amount to the suggestion that it is only self-indulgence which can be discovered to explain the chemist's decision, at least until more is said. It may amount, again, to a challenge to produce *a moral explanation* or *a moral reason*. We are indeed told that the unpleasant feelings which the chemist would have if he did the job would be 'emotional expressions of a thought that to accept would be wrong'.[21] However, we are not told the thought, or given to understand anything much about its nature.

What we seem to end with, then, if we look to what is said about 'integrity' in order to find a moral consideration or principle of relevance, is something different, the feeling that the imagined chemist would indeed only be engaged in a kind of self-indulgence.

Do we get further on toward finding a consideration or principle if we direct our attention to what is said about responsibility? To recall, it is allowed that the chemist is in some sense responsible for the research going forward more quickly than it might, since that, as he knows, is the upshot of his refusing to do it himself. However, he is said to be less reesponsible than he would be if

[20] *Op. cit.*, pp. 102-3.
[21] *Op. cit.*, p. 103.

he were to do it himself. He is less responsible in that a vital link is the other man's activity.

There is the possibility of having the wrong thing in mind here. Certainly the chemist's responsibility for research done by himself, *and*, as we can say, *freely chosen*, would be greater than his responsibility for the other man's research. What one should have in mind, presumably, is something else: what the chemist's responsibility would be if he himself went ahead with the research for the strong or indeed coercive reason that otherwise the other man would do it more efficiently. If the chemist did *that*, would he have a lesser responsibility than he has when he refuses the job?

In any case it is far from evident that the rightness of actions has to do with responsibility in such a way that the argument about the chemist is at all persuasive. Let us assume it to be a fact that the chemist in refusing the job is less responsible for the research than if he were to do it himself because of the coercive reason. Let us add in, for what it is worth, that in not taking the job he does not *make* the other man's research happen. Do we now have a consideration or a principle which might lead us to agree that he does the right thing in refusing the job?

I cannot see that here, or elsewhere, we find such a thing. It is essential to the argument, of course, that the consideration be produced. It would not be enough to suppose that it can be perceived, but not reported, by someone of especially good moral vision.

Finally and differently, notice that any moral consideration having to do with integrity or responsibility, supposing it can be found and got clear, is of fairly small importance. In a second example,[22] which involves a man's straight choice between killing one person and acting in such a way that someone else will kill twenty, it is allowed that the man's integrity and responsibility cannot stand in the way of his taking one life in order to save twenty.

In the case of the chemist, in fact, we are likely to attribute more weight to some consideration of integrity than we should. That is, if we feel inclined to side with the chemist in his decision, we may too quickly attribute this inclination to a consideration of

[22] *Op. cit.*, pp. 88–9.

integrity. This comes about, I think, because the case as described is indeterminate. Different possibilties are left open. This in fact brings it into line with reality, but, as can be seen on reflection, it also makes it indecisive as a proof or persuasion about integrity.

Very briefly, we have been assuming of the case that what the chemist should do, if he is to choose the state of affairs most likely to avoid distress and inequality, is to take the job, knowing he will do it less efficiently. But that is not entirely clear. One rightly takes it, in thinking of the situation, that there is only a probability that there will be a chemical and biological war to which the research will contribute. But *how small* a probability is in question? If we take it, unreflectively, to be *very* small, so that a war is in fact very improbable, then any inclination we have to side with the chemist may perhaps be explained by our consequential attitudes. That is, we may be moved by the consideration, as people generally are, that a possible upshot very unlikely to obtain must count for less than one which is certain or probable. What *is* certain or probable, if the chemist takes the job, is that he will be distressed, that he will not have registered a protest, and so on.[23]

It remains to transfer these conclusions from the example of the chemist, where attention is not likely to be led away from the principal question by passion or aversion, back to the subject of political violence. What I wish to suggest is that one response to violence and its agents, a response having to do with something other than consequences of actions, is at least unclear, and certainly not something of large moral importance. Whatever is to be said against violence, there appears to be no large argument to be found in suppositions of the kind we have considered, about integrity, responsibility, and hence about certain moral prohibitions.

6. IRRATIONALITY

Political violence is said to be irrational, and said so often enough that the opinion has a persuasiveness for that fact alone.

---

[23] Williams considers this sort of suggestion, that consequentalist attitudes may be seen as supporting the chemist's decision. His remarks, I think, do not really undercut the suggestion.

Let us consider the matter, which is in fact large and ramifying. That it *is* this, rather than something easily manageable, is much of what I wish to maintain.

Some lesser but bedevilling things need to be noticed before we come to what is of most consequence. First, it at least appears that a good deal of slipshod self-persuasion and perhaps persuasion of others goes forward in this area. Let us look at one example. Karl Popper, near the beginning of his essay on 'Utopia and Violence', which has to do with political violence as we have understood it and also with war, writes as follows:

> It. . .need not be a vain hope—that violence can be reduced, *and brought under the control of reason.*
>
> This is perhaps why I, like many others, believe in reason; why I call myself a rationalist. I am a rationalist because I see in the attitude of reasonableness *the only alternative* to violence.[24]

Near the end of the essay, following on a reflection of which I shall say a bit more, one which brings together 'rationalism' with a belief in human equality, and violence with a belief in inequality, there is this observation:

> Reason. . .is *the precise opposite* of an instrument of power and violence. . . .[25]

We are offered an explanation elsewhere in the essay of 'reason' or 'rationality' or 'reasonableness'. It is explained as a certain set of ways of ending disputes, ways which are related at least by the fact that they are all non-violent. They include give-and-take discussion, argument, arbitration, willingness to be convinced, willingness to admit error, and so on.

The sentences quoted may be taken to express sentiments of the right kind. However, they may also be looked at more critically,

---

[24] *Conjectures and Refutations: The Growth of Scientific Knowledge* (London, 1963), p. 355. For a related discussion of Popper, see Roy Edgley, 'Reason and Violence', in S. Körner, ed., *Practical Reason* (Oxford, 1974).

[25] *Op. cit.*, p. 363.

as indeed they should be. As may be confirmed by reading the essay, they do not have in them propositions which are argued for elsewhere. Still, they are not mere bluff declarations that 'reasonableness' is right and violence is wrong. They are more than that, which is not to say that they have argument in them.

(i) In part they are an instance of the simple enterprise of persuasion-by-naming. That is, one set of ways of ending disputes is given a good name or rather three good names. Of course, there is some warrant in ordinary language for using the mentioned terms for the defined ways of ending disputes. There is most warrant for naming them the ways of 'reasonableness'. It is a small fact, and of no use in serious reflection. As we shall see in a moment, it is perfectly possible to describe some violence as 'reasonable', 'rational', or as proceeding from 'reason'.

(ii) In part, the quoted sentences declare a fundamental opposition between violence and 'reasonableness', which opposition invites one toward a general judgement on violence. However, if one is to take the sentences seriously, one needs to know what opposed features of violence and 'reasonableness' are in question, and why these may be thought to make 'reasonableness' invariably right. These questions are not adequately answered, and so we are left without argument. In the place of adequate answers, there is the remarkably unsupported linking of 'reasonableness' with equality and violence with inequality, and perhaps one other relevant contribution. However, it can stand by itself for consideration.

(iii) That is, one may speculate that the quoted sentences also have in them this piece of persuasion. *'Reasonableness', which is give-and-take discussion and so on, is alone rational, the only choice for a rationalist. Hence it is always superior to violence, which is never rational.* What does the word 'rational' mean here? If we continue to take it to mean something about give-and-take discussion and so on, the proposition that reasonableness is rational is not a premise for the given conclusion or indeed anything much, since it is merely tautological. If no different and suitable meaning for 'rational' is given or suggested, we have only rhetoric.

Might the piece of persuasion be turned into something better? Elsewhere in the essay, Popper mentions in passing an entirely

familiar and indeed a fundamental conception of rationality. 'An
action is rational if it makes the best use of the available means
in order to achieve a certain end.'[26] Irrationality thus consists in
the adoption of means which do not in fact serve one's end, or
serve it at too great a cost. By the use of these conceptions we can
certainly escape tautology.

Is it obvious, however, as presumably it should be in the
absence of argument, that 'reasonableness' as defined is always
or generally rational, the best means to the end? It is not. Is
violence the precise opposite, whatever that may be, of rationality
in this sense? Is violence never the best means to the end? That is
obviously not obvious. As it happens, indeed, it is maintained by
Popper in the essay that a good deal of violence is *not* irrational
in the given sense, but rational.[27] That is, violence against those
who are intolerant or threaten violence is defended as the best
means. We thus come to a question about political violence rather
than a generalization to be used against it.

Before considering this major question, there are three other
distractions we may put aside quickly. One, which is also brought
to mind by 'Utopia and Violence', is the idea that violence is
unreasonable because it is the result of speculation about a utopia,
a transformed society. This speculation is poor stuff, and the
activity which follows from it is therefore ill-founded. One thing
to be said here is that it is plainly mistaken to suppose that all
political violence has to do with the large goal of a transformed
society. Most political violence has had smaller ends. It is equally
mistaken to run together all reflection which *does* have to do with
transformations of society. It is not all of the same quality or
kind. For example, not all of it has to do with speculative philosophy of history, as in Hegel and Marx.

The second distracting supposition is that the agents of violence
are figures of irrationality in that they are self-deceived. That is,
their actions are in fact not done from motives which have to do
with the facts of inequality. Their thoughts, and their protesta-
tions, are mistaken. What needs to be said about this is that it
would be a remarkable fact, one that would distinguish one kind
of human endeavour from all others, if those who engage in vio-

[26] *Op. cit.*, p. 358.
[27] *Op. cit.*, p. 357.

lence were *never* subject to anything but what they themselves take to be their ends. Equally, it would be remarkable if campaigns of violence with supposed political ends were ever wholly the product, or even in large part the product, of desires unrelated to those ends. It thus seems to me mistaken to suppose that senseless and unrecognized hostility, and like things, never have anything to do with campaigns of political violence, or, as we are told, that they often come near to composing them.

The third supposition also has to do with the agents of violence. It is not to be assumed, as often it seems to be, that their own views and defences of their conduct are the only possible views and defences. We do not suppose, generally, that what can be said for or against a line of action is no more than can be said by those persons who are or might be engaged in it. No such requirement survives reflection. No one would deny, certainly, that lines of action and their outcomes are in different ways determined by the beliefs and passions of the agents. Their beliefs and passions, then, must enter into anyone's consideration of the value of their conduct. This granted, it remains mistaken to fix on the agents and to suppose that political violence is to be seen only or precisely as those who are engaged in it do see it.

To turn now to the major subject-matter, what may come to mind is something like this question: *Is political violence generally irrational in that it gives rise to distress itself and yet is uncertain to achieve its ends?* It is all right as a question, but only as a culminating, final question. Something like it nonetheless appears to be the *only* question about irrationality which is considered by many philosophers who offer pronouncements. At any rate, they answer only it or something like it. What is certain is that any effective answer to so general and presupposing a question must be supported by explicit answers to quite a number of antecedent questions.

Violence differs considerably in its first effects and the same is true of its aims. One obvious essential, then, before answering the general question, appears to be a separation of kinds of violence in terms of first effects and aims or ends. Is the kind of political violence which will almost certainly consist only in damage to property, rather than injury or death, a rational means of pursuing equality, or greater equality, in lifetimes and in the quality of life? What of the kind of violence which carries a risk of a relatively small number of injuries or deaths, although it seeks to avoid them, and has the same end? What of the kind of violence, still with the same end, which consists in intentional injury? What of violence, again with the same end, which consists in intentionally causing death?

What of the rationality of violence of each of these kinds but with the different end of *political* equality? What of violence of each of these kinds but with the end not of *achieving* any of the mentioned kinds of equality, but the end of increasing the probability that these ends will be secured in a given time?

There is point in remarking that we can count sixteen questions here, and that more can be added, each of them independent and of importance. Indeed, before considering such additions, each of the sixteen questions needs to be replaced by several which are different in that they contain approximate numbers. Certainly such questions will be regarded as offensive by many, but they are far from unknown elsewhere in human life and they are certainly unavoidable.

Let us in what follows have in mind but one of them: *Is violence which causes several thousand injuries or deaths, despite attempts to avoid most of them, a rational means of pursuing equalities in lifetime and in quality of life for a society's worst-off tenth, numbering more than five million people?* It will be obvious enough to anyone who hesitates for reflection that we are far from being able to *assume* an answer. This has to do with the fact that the question also raises others.

Let us put aside problems having to do with uncertainty of outcome for a moment. We suppose, that is, that the violence in question would in fact produce the equalities. Would it be worth it? If we are familiar with the existence of such choices, where different kinds of things must be compared, we certainly are not familiar with a defensible way of answering them. This is partly a matter of fundamental principles, of which I shall have more to say in the last part of this essay. It is also partly a matter of judging the nature of kinds of human experience. There is no agreed method. We do not have a way of assessing injuries and deaths on the one hand and, on the other hand, the various inequalities and deprivations. We must somehow judge of such matters if we are to arrive at reasoned conclusions about the rationality of violence. Anyone who argues that some violence is rational must obviously deal with comparative questions of this kind. Anyone arguing that political violence is irrational must also do so, although not for so obvious a reason.

To take up what was put aside, the matter of uncertainty of outcome, I have already assumed in these remarks that it may be that some violence is rational even if it is not certain to succeed. Although sometimes those who condemn violence seem to suppose that it must always be certain of success in order to be rational, this is a proposition for which argument is needed. There obviously are circumstances in human life where something that is not certain to succeed, or even something that is unlikely to succeed, is rationally attempted. These, of course, are situations of greater or lesser extremity. Very roughly, then, there is the question of how probable it must be that the given violence will be successful if it is to be rational. The answer, which I shall certainly not try to give, will depend in good part on comparisons of the facts of violence and the facts of inequality.

The question will bring to mind yet another, which is as essential. Any view of the rationality of a kind of violence will depend on a factual judgement, more likely many such judgements, of the actual probability of success, as distinct from the probability necessary for rationality. What is to be said here will have much but not everything to do with the evidence of history. The same applies to the other relevant factual question of probability: How probable is it that given ends of political violence will or would be achieved by non-violent means?

These latter three questions, about uncertainty, are like the others in having presuppositions which must themselves be fixed. What period of time is to be assumed in the last question about achieving ends by non-violent means? That question, if made explicit, must mention a period in which the ends will or would be achieved. The fact of mortality, and hence the length of human lifetimes, suggest a period. I shall not pursue the matter, except to say that it is easier to argue against violence, from a premise about things being better for future generations as a result of non-violent progress, if one's place in a present generation is satisfactory.

Enough has been said to establish that the ready response to political violence which consists in abusing it as irrational is open to question, indeed open to may questions. What has been said, equally, establishes that any unreflective response which consists in the opposite thing, accepting violence as rational, is as jejune. One's conclusion, which there is much point in asserting, must be that the question is an open one.

Such a conclusion is likely to give rise to several different although related responses, which I shall not attempt to discuss adequately. One is that violence must be mistaken in that it causes harm or tragedy and *its rationality has not been shown.* If a general comment is of use here, it is that the choice is not necessarily one between violence, whose rationality is not established, and something else, whose rationality *is* established. There are the same kinds of difficulty to be faced in considering the alternative to violence: non-violent activity which appears to have a lesser chance of securing an acceptable change in the facts of inequality. Perhaps it does not need saying again that a different view, to the effect that this other political activity is already established as rational, is likely to derive in good part from an insufficient appreciation of the facts of inequality. A relevant generalization, obviously, is that situations of extremity do call for the consideration of the rationality of terrible means.

One other thing that may come to mind as a consequence of my conclusion about an open question is that accredited members of societies, as they might be called, are more able to guess what should be done about the facts of inequality. Accredited members include governments and their personnel, leaders of traditional political parties, and so on. Whatever one may think in general of the right of governments to take decisions, it may be supposed that they are in a superior position of knowledge, or of ignorance, when compared to those who contemplate or engage in political violence.

When this is a piece of unexamined piety, as often it is, perhaps there is room for that familiar jibe that the wars and catastrophes owed to the accredited members of society do not recommend their judgement. If we depart from piety, and from the jibe, we are bound to find difficulty rather than simplicity. Part of it has to do with the connections between power and judgement, or between power and want of judgement.[28]

My general conclusion here, then, is that common responses to political violence, having to do with its supposed irrationality, are themselves unreasonable. In the end, when the work of inquiry and reflection has been done, it may be that the strongest arguments against political violence will indeed be those having to do with the probabilities of success. No doubt we can conclude, now, that such arguments will sometimes be as conclusive as arguments in this area ever can be. No doubt there are many situations in which political violence cannot be justified, because it is sufficiently unlikely to work.

It may also become evident in the end, less comfortingly, that violence *would* be justified in these situations if it worked. That is, it may become evident that in these situations, as in others, violence which *did* secure change in inequalities would be preferable to no violence and no change. What may be thought to follow from such a proposition is not our concern now.

7. PRINCIPLES OF EQUALITY

Classical Utilitarianism as a basic morality appears to have had its day, and to have remaining to it only a twilight in economic theory. At the same time, as implied in the fifth section of this essay, it is impossible to leave out of morality a proposition to the effect that the distress of individuals is to be decreased, and, as a second priority, their satisfaction increased. The extent of each person's distress, and also the number of persons distressed, *must* be facts relevant to moral decisions about actions, policies, practices and whatever. What needs to be added to a proposition about distress, obviously, is something about equality. It is made necessary by the fact that the proposition about distress allows for inequality. That Classical Utilitarianism allows for inequality, and indeed calls for it in certain circumstances, is its familiar and fundamental weakness.

[28] Stuart Hampshire discusses and defends Bertrand Russell's relevant condemnation of governments in 'Russell, Radicalism, and Reason', in *Philosophy and Political Action* (London, 1972), edited by Virginia Held, Kai Nielsen and Charles Parsons.

What emerges, although far from clearly, is that what we must have is a principle or a pair or a set of principles which give importance to the avoidance of both distress and inequality. These principles would be directed, so to speak, to what can be named the ideal of equal wellbeing. The need for such principles, or such a principle, would also emerge, incidentally, from an attempt to rely solely on a principle of equality. Obviously, a perfect equality of suffering leaves much to be desired. What we must also have, in addition to the fundamental principle or principles, although this is not our present concern, are subordinate conceptions, rules and so on. One of these, to give a single example, would have to do with forms of government. These latter things would be consequences of the fundamental principles.

To announce these needs, however, is to say something less than wonderfully useful. While the conviction that we should have such fundamental principles is not uncommon, we have not got them. I do not mean that they have not yet been put in decent order, although that appears to me to be true.[29] Rather, the point is that we do not have them in place within our own thinking. As a consequence we find ourselves in *some* confusion about what I have called the facts of inequality. So it is, or should be, with the facts of violence and with any conclusion about its justification.

To provide the basic principles would be to provide the most important one of the reasonings, as they were called above in the third section of this essay, which stand between premises of fact and substantial conclusions about violence. The full and final devising of the principles cannot be our present business. Let us finish, rather, by reflecting a bit on the difficulty of the enterprise and hence the difficulty of emerging from the mentioned confusion about the facts of inequality and of violence. Are we, as some suppose, in so much or such deep difficulty about principles that a kind of despair is in place, an acceptance of early defeat in our reflections and of what follows from it?

There are problems, certainly, with any large proposition about the avoidance of distress. These are usually discussed in connection with Utilitarianism. There are also thought to be difficulties in

[29] An extended attempt has been made by John Rawls in *A Theory of Justice* (Oxford, 1972). A principal part of his doctrine is discussed in the second essay of this book.

the other part of the enterprise, pertaining to equality. It is these at which I should like to look. They arise in the course of attempting to settle one's mind about equality itself, and hence *before* the stage at which considerations of equality and the avoidance of distress are brought together, and a kind of compromise is struck.

If one picks up a piece of philosophical writing on equality, there is a decent chance that it will describe equalitarian thinking, by which I mean the propounding and defending of principles of equality, as weak, or as incoherent, or as lacking a defensible and substantial principle, or as coming to very little in the end.[30] These claims are independent of the point already noticed, that principles of equality must finally be brought into conjunction with something else. A pastiche derived from these philosophical writings on equality, a decently representative one, goes as follows.

Consider the *Principle of Absolute Equality,* which is that everyone is to be treated absolutely equally in every respect. This is absurd. It is absurd because, for example, not everyone can possibly live by the seaside. Also, we cannot think of treating the sick as we treat the healthy. If more needed to be said of the principle, there is the fact that there is no earthly chance of its being realized, and that if it were realized, the resulting dull uniformity would be appalling.

[30] The following recent writings, while of different kinds, qualities and sympathies, share at least the feature of overlooking what I call The Principle of Equality: S. I. Benn and R. S. Peters, *Social Principles and the Democratic State* (London, 1959), Chapter Five; W. T. Blackstone, 'On the Meaning and Justification of the Equality Principle', *Ethics,* 1967; Norman E. Bowie, 'Equality and Distributive Justice', *Philosophy,* 1970; John Charvet, 'The Idea of Equality as a Substantive Principle of Society', *Political Studies,* 1969; J. R. Lucas, *The Principles of Politics* (Oxford, 1966), Section 56, and 'Against Equality', *Philosophy,* 1965; Felix E. Oppenheim, 'Egalitarianism as a Descriptive Concept', *American Philosophy Quarterly,* 1970; D. D. Raphael, *Problems of Political Philosophy* (London, 1970), pp. 183–94; John Rees, *Equality* (London, 1971), Chapters Seven and Eight; Nicholas Rescher, *Distributive Justice* (Indianapolis, 1966), Chapter Four; Bernard Williams, 'The Idea of Equality', in Peter Laslett and W. G. Runciman, editors, *Philosophy, Politics and Society,* Second Series (Oxford, 1962).

D

Let us, then, be guided by the idea just mentioned, that obviously the sick are not to be treated equally with the well. Indeed the only sensible thinking about equality begins from the observable facts that men are different or unequal in some respects and perhaps the same or equal in other respects. The sensible general idea of equality, in fact, is that those who are in fact equal in a certain respect ought to be treated equally, and those who are in fact unequal ought to be treated unequally. This is the *Principle of Formal Equality.*

If it derives from Aristotle, however, it does not carry us at all far. It gives no direction at all until one has found what actual equalities do exist among men. Clearly they are not equal in intelligence, industry and a great deal else. Indeed, it seems that they *are* equal *only* in having certain basic or fundamental needs and desires, and if one can ever get the matter clear, in being *individuals.* That is, perhaps, they are such that they should be treated as ends rather than means.

Given the overwhelming natural differences or inequalities between men, and these few equalities, it is merely confusion to suppose that men ought in *many* respects to be treated equally. Nothing of this kind follows from the Principle of Formal Equality. The most that one can reasonably say is that they ought to be treated equally in such basic ways as these: all should have their fundamental needs and desires satisfied, and none should be deprived of what is called human respect.

We may take this consequence of the second principle and regard it as a principle by itself, that of *Minimal Equality.* It does not require anything like a large redistribution of wealth, or greater participation in social decisions, or an end of social distinctions. It does not require much. What it comes to is something far less than equalitarians have imagined. There is in fact no large and defensible principle of equality.

Equalitarians have also offered many other principles. There is the *Principle of Equal Opportunity* and there is the Principle of *Equality of Wealth.* They have claimed too, if not often, that those who are of *equal merit* should be treated equally, and that those of *equal need* should be treated equally. The latter principle, sometimes expressed as 'to each according to his need', implies the existence of unequal needs, and so is not the Principle of Minimal Equality.

These principles taken together are inconsistent. Equal opportunity issues in inequality of wealth. When these inconsistencies are seen, something must in any case be given up, but how is the Equalitarian to choose? Moreover, it is quite unclear how these latter principles are related to the previous two, those of Formal Equality and Minimal Equality.

If the foregoing sketch were truly a sketch of the best that can be done with notions of equality, we would have some reason for being intellectually dismayed by the prospect of trying to get some moral grip on the state of our societies, on the facts of inequality. However, the situation is otherwise. What follows is only a part of what might be said.

Is there really no general and substantial principle of equality, no unqualified ideal which is fundamental to equalitarian feeling, and which would enter into the construction of a basic morality? The first principle mentioned in the sketch, that everyone is to be treated equally in every respect, is certainly unqualified. This, however, the Principle of Absolute Equality, *is* indeed nonsense. It is also nonsense, though, to suggest that it is all that is possible by way of an unqualified ideal.

Notice that it is a principle about *treatment*: that is, roughly, what is to be *done for* and *done to* people. To fix on the idea of treatment is to miss something else that is at the very bottom of ordinary thought about equality. It is, roughly, the variegated *experience* of individuals, or the qualities of the experience of individuals. These qualities, still to speak generally, come together into satisfaction or distress, wellbeing or illbeing. There is then what has the right to be called, simply, *The Principle of Equality*. In one form it is that there is a presumption that everyone should be equal in satisfaction and distress. It is, again, that things should be so arranged that we approach as close as we can, which may not be all that close, to equality in satisfaction and distress. The principle's further formulation and its defence lead

one toward certain familiar problems, and indeed into them, but
at bottom it is reassuringly simple. It lies behind one's being
appalled by the great differences in lifetimes with which we
began, although it is not all that explains one's response.

This principle does not carry the inane consequence that we
must treat everyone alike, the sick with the well. Nor, to return
to the frivolous example of the seaside, does it have the overwhelming practical disability of the Principle of Absolute Equality. That is, it does not run up against the truth that certain
large physical impossibilities stand in the way of equal treatment.
The Principle of Equality does not have these consequences,
because of differences between individuals. Since everyone's going
to the seaside is not a condition of equal satisfaction, we should
not have to have everyone at the seaside to realize the principle.
Again, since individuals are different, they can obviously be equal
in satisfaction without living the same and producing a flat uniformity.

It may be objected to The Principle of Equality that there is
no earthly possibility of the realization of the ideal which it in-
corporates. That may or may not be true, but let us say that it is.
The Principle of Equality, then, is like other principles and ideals.
It obviously does not follow that it should not direct our efforts.
As we know, incidentally, it cannot be supposed that it is *all* that
should direct our efforts. To mention too briefly the pertinent
argument, equality of distress in a society is not preferable to an
inequality of satisfaction.

Another objection may be expected from many philosophers.
They are those who have assumed, with Aristotle, that all
principles of equality necessarily rest on natural or factual
equalities and inequalities. They have assumed that one must
find an equality of fact, perhaps intelligence, in order to *justify*
an equality of treatment.

There is no such general requirement and certainly there is no
such requirement on The Principle of Equality. Indeed, to think
one is in place appears to require some confusion with an
obscure aesthetic principle, having to do with symmetry, or perhaps some speculation that we must act in accordance with the
instructions of a god, instructions which he has made implicit in
his creation. The Principle of Equality, if anything does, stands

as self-recommending in moral thought. It does presuppose certain similar potentialities in all men, which is an entirely different matter from finding a justification in these similarities. It directs our attention not to factual *equalities* but rather to factual *inequalities*. We are not to mimic factual equalities but rather to compensate for factual inequalities.

To return to the sketch, and to the Principle of Formal Equality, it should now be clear that we have no need to search out sufficient similarity between men so as to secure the small conclusion that fundamental needs and desires should be satisfied and that persons should be accorded a certain respect. That is, we need not struggle toward and end with the Principle of Minimal Equality. We already have a principle which secures the things in question and also a great deal more.

This is not to say that there is no place for anything like the Principle of Formal Equality. Something quite like it follows as a consequence from The Principle of Equality, as was implied a moment ago in what was said about the seaside and dull uniformity. Given that one wants to secure or maintain equal satisfaction, it follows that if two persons are *equally satisfied*, then *equal treatment* is in order. If they are *unequally satisfied* then *unequal treatment* is in order. The Principle of Equality also has certain more particular consequences which bring to mind the Principle of Formal Equality. If we wish to secure something like equality of satisfaction, it will be right in certain cases to treat equally, in some respect, those who are in fact equal in an ability, or a need, or health, or some other particular respect. Such rules tend to be in the forefront of political discussion and activity, and The Principle of Equality, in *explicit* form, is not much in evidence. It is plain, nonetheless, that the rules have their origin or ground in the principle.

To return for one more moment to the sketch, it can certainly be allowed that in working out the equalitarian part of a basic morality, or, better, in working toward a basic morality by way of equalitarian attitudes, one will certainly have to deal with conflicts between secondary principles of equality. Obviously, the principle of equal opportunity does sometimes conflict with other things. However, it is only if one has a remarkably simple view of human existence, and is forgetful of an immense amount of moral and religious reflection, that it will come as a surprise that principles do conflict, and some must be discarded. It is no cause for despair. What one needs to do is something which is possible, some decision-making, guided in part by The Principle of Equality.

There would be no point in going only a little way further here with these reflections. I shall have something more to say of basic principles in the next essay of this book. What I wish to suggest here is that in considering the facts of inequality, or, as they might as rightly be called, the facts of distress, we are not at sea. In particular, while it would be footling to suggest that there are no problems, we are not so confused about basic principles as to be unable to make a decent response. It is not that the facts of inequality, or of violence, must defeat moral theory and commit us to a passivity of judgement.

2

On Two Pieces of Reasoning About Our Obligation to Obey the Law

All of us, save some true anarchists, have the conviction that the members of a society have some obligation to abide by its laws. At any rate, there is this obligation if the society is at all tolerable, which is to say that it has risen above barbarism, ancient or modern. Many things are not to be done, for a reason having to do with the fact that they are illegal, as distinct from other reasons which may also exist. It is thought by some that this obligation to keep to the laws is at its strongest with respect to the laws prohibiting violence. Still, it is quite unclear from what it is that the general obligation derives, and hence what weight it has. Almost all of us accept the existence of *political obligation*, as it happens to be called, since it may also be expressed as an obligation to the state or to government. Still, we are likely to grant that there are circumstances even in tolerable and better societies when the obligation is rightly over-ridden.

Of the long welter of doctrines whose aim has been to maximize or to minimize the fact of political obligation, I should like to consider two which are recent and, it might be said, culminating. Both are developed reasonings of the kind mentioned in passing in the first essay of this book.[1] The first is partly to the effect that to accept political obligation, understood in a certain way, is in fact to be immoral. It is to go against a certain moral imperative. The second is partly to the effect that political obligation, differently understood, must be recognized as weighty. While

[1] See above, pp. 11–12.

one may in extraordinary circumstances be enabled to escape the obligation to the extent of engaging in the mildness of civil disobedience, or in what is called conscientious refusal, anything more is as good as unthinkable.

The first doctrine, owed to Robert Paul Wolff and understandably the subject of a certain amount of controversy, comes of one of the traditions of thought and feeling which give first place to conscience and individual responsibility, and second place to political obligation and the like.[2] What is said about the immorality of political obligation is taken to have consequences for a particular idea of violence, one called the distinctive political concept of violence. We shall consider that matter, which is intimately related, as well.

The second doctrine, owed to John Rawls and very much discussed by philosophers, derives from the tradition which has to do with suppositions about a social contract and about obligations which flow from it.[3] However, it is different from all or many of its predecessors. One large difference is that we are offered not only an argument about political obligation, and in particular our obligation not to use violence, but also an argument for two basic moral principles for the ordering of societies.

We shall not ignore the second argument since it is, in fact, of direct relevance to one of the fundamental difficulties encountered in reflection on political violence. This is the difficulty, of which something was said at the end of the first essay in this book, of settling on basic moral principles. We shall, then, consider not only certain specific contentions about a social contract

[2] Robert Paul Wolff, 'On Violence', *Journal of Philosophy*, 66 (1969), pp. 601–16; *In Defence of Anarchism* (New York, 1970). One commentary on Wolff's work is *In Defence of Political Philosophy* New York, 1972), by Jeffrey H. Reiman.

[3] John Rawls, *A Theory of Justice* (Oxford, 1972). Most of the book is not unlike Rawls's earlier essays. These include 'Justice as Fairness', in *Philosophy, Politics and Society*, Second Series, ed. Peter Laslett and W. G. Runciman (Oxford, 1962) pp. 132–57; 'Distributive Justice', in *Philosophy, Politics and Society*, Third Series, ed. Laslett and Runciman (Oxford, 1969), pp. 58–82; '*The Justification of Civil Disobedience*,' in *Civil Disobedience: Theory and Practice*, ed. Hugo Adam Bedau (New York, 1969), pp. 240–255.

and political obligation but also the argument for two basic moral principles, and the principles themselves.

Finally, by way of introduction to these two doctrines, it is to be said that they appear in one respect similar. They are complex, if in different ways. Their complexity, if I am right, is a false one. The fundamental argument, in each case, is relatively simple in kind, however compelling or uncompelling. An examination of the two doctrines, then, may serve to engender or strengthen a certain scepticism about what might be described as The Impressive in political argument. This scepticism, I am sure, in consideration of violence and other matters of seriousness, is an essential. Matters of seriousness call for a certain kind of attention, and they generally have in them quite enough of true and unavoidable complexity. Certainly this is true of political violence.

My intentions in summary, then, are to consider a rejection of political obligation, to consider an acceptance of it and a related argument for two moral principles, and to raise a scepticism. The smallest intention is not the last one. To try to realize it, I shall linger a bit at points in the discussion rather than press on singlemindedly.

1. A RIGHT TO OBEDIENCE

Wolff's essay 'On Violence' has to do with the idea, as it may be expressed, and as he does express it, that some governments or states have *authority*. Some governments or states, to put the same thing differently, have a right to be obeyed by their subjects, the members of the relevant societies. This appears to be tantamount to the proposition which is our concern, that the subjects have an obligation to obey the law.

The obligation depends on the existence of law, as already remarked, and hence also on the existence of government and presumably society. The *reason* for the obligation has to do essentially with law, government and society. Political obligation, so-called on this account, is thus distinct from other obligations. If a man wounds another, in most circumstances, it will be at least possible that he has broken two obligations. One, we may say, is the simple obligation not to wound others. He would have this obligation even in a 'state of nature'. He would have it, that is, even if there were no law, in the ordinary sense, against his action. In addition to this, there is what is relevant to our present reflections, his obligation not to break the law against wounding others.

Political obligation is obviously a kind of moral obligation, although not the most familiar kind. The idea is that the subjects of governments, or some governments, are under some moral obligation to give up all courses of action which are made illegal. There is a moral restraint or prohibition on subjects with respect to these courses of action which are prohibited by the law of the state. Subjects are in some degree constrained to give up the behaviour in question, despite the fact that some of it may be morally desirable in their view.

The idea that subjects have an obligation, that governments have an authority, has been defended in different ways in the history of political thought. A conclusion about authority is accepted today by those of us who are committed, happily or unhappily and more or less completely, to a kind of government described by ourselves as democratic and by some others as bourgeois-democratic. It has been accepted by those who have made use of the notion of a social contract, as we know, by those who have believed in a monarch's divine right to rule, and by those who have found a superiority for a social or an economic class in the wisdom of the class or in what may be called its historical role or mission.

There is a good deal more to be said about the nature of political obligation, but let us now pass on to a second thing in 'On Violence'. The *distinctive political concept of violence*, like other concepts of violence, is said to be an idea of a use of force to effect decisions against the desires of others. That all concepts of violence have these features seems mistaken, but the matter is not important. The special feature of distinctively political violence is that it is a use of force either prohibited or not authorized (we are offered these two different possibilties) *by a state which has authority*. It is a use of force prohibited, to remain with that possibility, by a state whose subjects are under an obligation to obey its commands.

Let us look, thirdly, at a very different claim which enters into the argument. It is one to which Immanuel Kant gave some attention in his moral philosophy, and it is that a man is under an obligation not to act in a given way unless he himself sees good reason for so doing. The principal part of what is meant here is that a man is obliged not to act on the mere ground that someone has told him to do so. I do not have a reason for action in the bare fact that someone has told me to do whatever it is.

This seems a defensible claim, although it is inexplicit as it stands, and perhaps is in need of qualification. If we were to consider qualification, we should have to look into the possibility that unless we are all to become a good deal more reflective than we are, or more inactive, the range of acts in question must be limited. Humming a bit of a song while walking across a field with someone may not seem to be something that requires any reason. Certainly I am not prohibited from doing so by the fact that all I have in the forefront of my mind is that my companion has asked me to do the thing. Or, should we say that one's unconsidered recognition that certain behaviour is inconsequential *does* provide one with a good reason for the behaviour? In any case there is also consequential behaviour to consider. If I lack the slightest notion of what will avert some disaster, I am surely permitted to do what I am told by someone who has a gleam of hope in his eye. I am under no obligation not to act. Given these several reflections, it seems that a man can fulfil his obligation and still come pretty close to doing something simply because he has been told to do it.

There is more to be said, but let us now assemble our three pieces, unfinished as they are, and see how they work. There is an obligation just mentioned not to perform many actions, or many actions in certain settings, without what seems to be a good reason. This excludes doing many things simply because one has been told to do them. Well then, no state or government can have authority, the authority mentioned above. There is an obligation borne by every man which makes it impossible for any state to possess a certain right to a man's obedience. Or rather, to include a qualification to which we shall return, no state which is a practical possibility can ever have the right in question. It is allowed that it might be possessed by a certain ideal democratic state— ideal in that all its policies are considered and voted on by all its citizens and hence have their unanimous support. Such a state is allowed to be a fantasy.

If no state that is practically possible can have the given right to a man's obedience, there are consequences for the distinctive political concept of violence. If violence is taken to be a use of force prohibited by a state with the authority in question, then there is no violence, since there is no such state to prohibit anything. No use of force falls under the distinctive political concept of violence. The concept is empty. In order to get to a still further conclusion that is drawn, that talk of violence of this kind is *incoherent*, one notices the presupposition that the concept does distinguish between uses of force that are violent and uses of force that are not. This is a presupposition of an entirely general kind, present in the use of any concept. However, by the argument just given, the concept we are considering fails to do any such distinguishing. No use of force is violent. Here we have incoherence, presumably related to inconsistency. Given the further argument that I intend, there will be no need for greater precision on this obscure point.

Incidentally, one can also attempt to establish the conclusion about incoherence from the other definition of violence. There, to recall, it is a use of force *not authorized*, as distinct from *prohibited*, by a state with the right kind of authority. In this case, since every use of force is *not authorized* by such a state, there being no such state, we may try to maintain that *every* use of force, however 'official', is an instance of violence, and also maintain the further conclusion about incoherence. Let us continue to have in mind the other form of the argument, proceeding from the definition of violence as a *prohibited* use of force.

2. CLARIFICATIONS

What we now have is less than crystal clear. Still, it is clear enough that the argument so far does not have as its goal a merely conceptual point, a point about the emptiness of incoherence of a concept. To describe the argument this way, at any rate, is entirely misleading. Its goal, rather, is a proposition of morality. The argument so far, at bottom, is something like this:

1. Each of us is obliged never to act, except perhaps in certain circumstances, on the mere ground that we have been told to do so.
2. Therefore, it is mistaken to think that any existing government could have a certain right to the obedience of its subjects.
3. One cannot claim, then, against those who do such things as set bombs, that they are violating a related obligation of obedience.

There is no reason to rewrite this latter conclusion in any less overt way. Consider an analogy. Suppose that one comes to believe, along with those impressed by the privacy of the soul, that it is impossible ever to assess a man's responsibility for an action. Suppose one believes, too, that it is necessary, if punishing a man is to be morally tolerable, that it be known that he was in fact responsible to some degree for an offence. There follows the conclusion that no one ought to be punished, whatever else we ought to do about criminal behaviour. The conclusion, for all that has been said so far, can be couched differently, by specifying a distinctive concept of *justified punishment*. Such punishment, we say, is of an offender of whom it is known that he was responsible for his offence. The conclusion of our bit of argument may then be put as this: the concept of a justified punishment applies to nothing and talk which makes use of it is incoherent.

There is in fact no reason to conclude this argument by somewhat obscuring observations on the concept of justified punishment. There is no more reason to conclude the other argument by talk of the distinctive political concept of violence. Some may think that this opinion can be supported by showing that neither the concept of justified punishment nor the given concept of violence is entrenched in ordinary usage or in any other relevant usage. This may be true. A better reason is that the guiding intention of both arguments is not merely to change usage—supposing such an achievement by itself to be even conceivable—but to contribute to a change in attitude, policy, and action. Given this, what might be called the standard form for moral judgement is preferable.

Let us then consider the argument in its direct and overt

expression, as set out a moment ago. What we have in the
first part is that a man is obliged never to act, except perhaps in
certain circumstances, simply because someone has told him to do
so. The concern of this nostrum is clearly the moral agent or the
good man. A good man, we feel, is one who has the trait among
others that he does not act without seeing good reason for doing
so. He acts in accordance with some fact of personal responsibility,
a fact which is not to be escaped and which he does not attempt to
escape. We must, it seems, accept the first item of the argument.

It is thought to follow from this that governments are not
justified in claiming a right of obedience from their subjects. They
cannot, we are told, have authority. Does this follow? Well, it
depends on how the thing is taken. It seems likely that there is
some right, *some* authority, which we must agree a government
cannot have if we accept the first part of the argument. Let us
settle clearly what particular authority it is that suits the argument. Let us see what kind of authority it is that a government
cannot have if the first part of the argument is accepted. Again,
what right of obedience is it that a government cannot have if we
accept that every man has an obligation not to act, anyway in
most circumstances, on the mere ground that he has been told to
do so?

To proceed a bit indirectly, let us imagine someone who does
not have the specified trait of the good man or the moral agent.
Imagine a man who is wholly law-abiding and who says that he
lives as he does only because the law so directs him. That, he
says, is good enough for him. If we pester him a bit, he will *not*
assent to various alternative arguments for his living as he does.
He will not accept the account that he lives as he does because
that is the lawful way *and* the law expresses his own will. Nor
does it matter to him, if it is true, that the law expresses the will
of a majority of the members of his society. He will not accept,
either, that a justification of his behaviour is that obedience to the
law has the recommendation that it avoids greater losses, of whatever kind, than those that may be involved in disobedience. If he
did assent to *any* such explanation of his conduct, he would not
be the man we want, not a pure case of the obligation of the
special kind that we have in mind.

We may suppose, if we want, that our man sometimes thinks

there is a good reason for obeying this or that law, a reason other than that it *is* a law. At other times, he thinks there is such a reason for not obeying a law. None of this makes any difference to him. His life, or the part of it with which we are concerned, is governed by the simple fact of his beliefs as to legality and illegality. If something is ordered by law, he does it. He is amoral, indeed what we might call the automatic law-abider, or, just conceivably, he is a man of *one* moral principle. It is, simply, that one ought to abide by the law, and absolutely. He has *no* other relevant moral belief. What gives rise to action on his part is the law, and, it must be remembered, this is not to be taken as involving an enthymeme. It is not that obeying the law has this or that further recommendation, as people often believe.

It is such a man, and only such a man, who does accord to his government the authority or right to obedience that fits the argument. It is such a man, and only such a man, who accords to his government an authority that runs against the obligation of which Kant speaks. The authority in question, now that it is more explicit, can be seen to be an extremely curious right, not merely to behaviour but to a certain genesis of behaviour. It is a right to unreflective responses or, as one might fairly say, to a certain sort of person.

3. A CONCESSION AND ITS IMPORTANCE

There remains a good deal of mystery about our man and the related authority that a government might be claimed to have. One would face great troubles in attempting to give a full characterization of what we can call the *unreflectively obedient man*. He may indeed be a phantasm of the philosophical imagination. In any case, it does seem necessary to agree, and not merely because of Kant's obligation, that it would be wrong for any government to have the authority in question. It is morally mistaken to think that any government could be justified in claiming *this* right of obedience from its subjects. The second step of the argument is certainly all right.

Most important, to pass on to the third step of the argument, we may grant without hesitation that there is one thing that *cannot* be said against the man who sets a bomb. It is that he has violated an obligation deriving from the government's right to his unreflective obedience. More simply, we cannot condemn him for not having been unreflectively or, as might be said, mindlessly obedient. We could only condemn him, it seems, if we took to be praiseworthy, or possibly praiseworthy, a different man: the soldier who kills the peasants without reflecting on what he does and *simply because* his officer has given him a command. We certainly do not regard either the automatic soldier, or the soldier with a single moral principle about obeying all commands, as praiseworthy.[4]

One incidental point is worth a moment before we press on. We were given to understand, before we became clearer about the authority in question, that it *could* be possessed by a government in an ideally democratic state. That is, subjects of that state could accord the authority to their government without infringing their Kantian obligation. This is confusion. What is true, rather, is that it is near enough a logical impossibility that the subjects of this state infringe their Kantian obligation. This is a state where all subjects consider, vote on, and in fact approve of all legislation. Given that, their obedience to law cannot count as unreflective obedience. The fact that I participate in making the laws, and agree to them, does not make it morally tolerable to obey them unreflectively. On the contrary, unless I am bizarrely divided personality, my participation makes it a logical impossibility. The confusion of thinking otherwise points to a fact to which we shall come.

Our present position is that we have conceded the force of an argument against a supposed obligation of obedience, and hence

---

[4] *Can* this concession be expressed even covertly as the concession that the distinctive political concept of violence is empty and that talk which uses it is incoherent? Is there no sense in talk of a use of force prohibited by a government which has a right to unreflective obedience? Well, we can *conceive* of a government which is in fact accorded a right it ought not to have. We can conceive, further, that it puts the usual prohibitions on certain uses of force. There are more problems here. The substantial conclusion of the argument is preserved in the overt form given above, however, so let us stick to that. I mean the proposition that the violent cannot be condemned for failing in a certain obligation, for going against a certain authority.

against a particular claim about a government's authority. There can be no such obligation on the part of those who contemplate violence, and no such authority on the part of a government which attempts to stop them. What is in question, as we have seen, is an authority of a striking kind. How important, then, is this concession?

It is said that people do in fact persist in assigning to the state precisely the authority which we have conceded that it cannot have. They have the belief, it is said, that the state has a right to what we have called unreflective obedience. Is this so? It seems to me impossible to think so. Does *anyone* believe that the state has *this* right? Does anyone believe the state has the right about whose nature we have become clear? There is no sense, of course, in supposing they have some *related* belief. A *related* belief might be acceptable and not be open to rejection by way of Kant's conception of the good man. Hence it would not fit the argument we have been considering.

It may be that many people have had, or indeed now have, attitudes to the state which are *consonant* with a demand for unreflective obedience, as understood above. Assuredly the state has been made an object of a kind of superstition, has been perceived as having a religious character or something akin to one, and has been offered something like worship. The attitudes owe something to the nature of governments. They make laws, and these are not seen as the giving of advice or the offering of reasons for certain conduct. Laws, it seems, are imperatives. One does not get, in a statute, a lot of reflection on why it ought to be obeyed. Hence, some may suppose, the implicit stand or position of governments is as follows: Do this because our enacted law demands it.

Still, it is pretty clear that these attitudes of veneration fall well short of the belief that the state has a right to unreflective obedience, that a man who sets a bomb is behaving wrongly because he has had some thoughts about his behaviour. It is therefore difficult to resist this first substantial conclusion of our reflections: *the argument we have been considering consists in refuting a quite deplorable belief ascribed to the opponents of political violence but unlikely ever to have been contemplated by them.*

There is another matter, perhaps more important. It may be

E

supposed that whether or not anyone has held to the belief, it nonetheless *is* essential or important to an argued opposition to violence. Hence, its failure is crucial. My second substantial conclusion, which I shall support in three ways, is that none of this is correct either. *That the belief is deplorable and refutable is something without further consequences. It is not a belief important to an argued opposition to violence.*

(i) In recognizing one claim about political authority as deplorably mistaken, we do not commit ourselves to any general view about the impossibility of ascribing any authority to the state. We are certainly not committed to thinking that there is *no* sort of authority or right to obedience that the state can have. We are not committed to thinking that there can be *no* arguments against violence which rest on the existence of society and government, and on a claim they make.

The idea that as a result of the given argument we cannot ascribe *any* authority to the state, which would be important, might arise from the supposition that to accord someone a right to something, or to grant someone authority with respect to some matter, *is* to grant an unquestionable power of decision. This is mistaken, as can certainly be shown.

What needs to be pointed out is that there is a notion of authority that is quite different, a notion that is in no way jeopardized by anything conceded so far. It is also clear, and it is what most or many readers will have had in mind at the beginning of this essay. If I think there is a moral argument for complying with most of a government's commands, and I also think that there exists certain kinds of expectation or support, I may with perfect sense talk of the government's right to obedience. The expectation is on the part of the government and society, and is an expectation of obedience to the government's commands. The support, in part, is support for the government in its attempt to enforce obedience to the commands. For the government to have this right is for it to have authority, indeed authority in the most common sense. It is an authority which can be had without its possessor being taken as godlike.

By way of illustration, suppose that I am a democrat in a democracy. I do not think that any policy the government may pass into law ought to be complied with, but I do think, for various reasons, that *some recommendation* attaches to supporting any policy that is passed into law, although there may be things against it. My central idea is that supporting the policy is supporting the system, which I take to be the best system of government. Quite often, I will vote for policy A over policy B and think it right to do so. However, if B wins over A, I will conduct myself according to B. Further, I will take the view that there are better reasons for complying with B, as a law, than A, supposing A to be against the law.

Thus there is, in my view, a moral argument for obedience to any democratically-enacted law. If others take this view and if there then exists the expectation and support mentioned above, it will be perfectly reasonable to talk of the government's right to obedience, the government's authority. This, incidentally, will be perfectly compatible with the belief that for *some* A and *some* B, there would be better reasons for complying with A, as a policy against the law, than B, supposing it to be the law.

These are perfectly ordinary conceptions of right and authority. It is clear that they need a good deal of attention, that they raise problems of several kinds. Equally clearly, we can anticipate that it in no way follows, from the fact that a government cannot have a right to unreflective obedience, that it cannot have authority at all. Most important, it does not follow that we cannot ever condemn the man who sets a bomb as having done something against the law, something prohibited by the government as a matter of right or authority.

Perhaps to put the point in that way is to obscure it, or to obscure it for some. The point does not have to do, fundamentally, with the propriety of talking precisely of *rights to obedience* and *authority*. We may feel little inclination to engage in such talk. Indeed, it may be thought that it is talk worth avoiding. The important thing is that there remains open the possibility of argument against violence which depends essentially on the existence of law, society and government, whether or not this argument mentions authority or rights. It can be argued, from several premises, that it is right or that there is a moral reason for obeying the law and hence refraining from violence. The fact that talk of rights and authority is in place (since others are likely to agree, and to give support) is of secondary importance.

(ii) A related idea about an important loss that we suffer, when we give up the specified argument against violence, has to do with the history of political theory. It does appear to be an assumption in 'On Violence' that traditional political theory has had as its principal object the establishing of a government's right to unreflective obedience.[5] It is assumed, it seems, that those who have maintained theories of a social contract, or those who have developed democratic theory, have been attempting to establish that each of a state's subjects has that obligation of obedience which is in conflict with the moral rule about having good reason for action. Hence, one may be led to the idea that all of traditional political theory has nothing of value to say against violence, since traditional political theory is argument for unreflective obedience, which is indefensible. An arsenal of argument has been shown to be empty.

However, it is a spectacular unlikelihood that Locke, for example, was concerned to argue for unreflective obedience. He was concerned, rather, to advance a reason for obedience. This should not be confused with anything else and, in particular, not with a reason for giving up reflection on the government's commands. It seems that Locke's contention included nothing whatever to which Kant could object. Precisely the same is true of other doctrines of authority which have places in the history of political thought. It does not matter that some of these doctrines come close to demanding *absolute* obedience. In fact, to suppose that the traditional political thinkers were struggling toward a proof of the rightness of *unreflective* obedience is to suppose them pretty well out of touch. We must see them as spending a long time giving us reasons for obeying the government, in the hope that we shall forget them.

Scholarship is not required for the main point, however. It is plain that the traditional political doctrines *can* be used in a

---

[5] We are told that 'claims to authority', the authority related to unreflective obedience, 'have been defended on a variety of grounds, most prominent among which are the appeal to God, to tradition, to expertise, to the laws of history, and to the consent of those commanded' ('On Violence', p. 603). Later (p. 612) it seems to be assumed that the argument of the essay has shown 'the classical theory of political authority' to be mistaken.

certain way. Whatever use may have been made of them, they *can* be used to argue for a familiar right of a government to obedience, a right of the kind mentioned a moment ago, something to be sharply distinguished from the right to unreflective obedience. For example, there are the arguments to the effect that a democratic governmnt is superior in several respects to a dictatorship. One can proceed, in particular, toward the conclusion that there is much to be said against violence, conceived fundamentally as a use of force that has been prohibited.

(iii)   There is one other idea that may come to mind in connection with the supposed seriousness of the concession about unreflective obedience. It is perhaps a more natural idea than either of its predecessors. As we have seen, there are a number of arguments which may issue in the conclusion that the state has *an* authority, *a* right to obedience, ordinarily conceived. On many occasions, it may be felt, this conclusion will carry the day over any other consideration. Certainly it will often carry the day over a man's sincere conviction that he ought to do what the state forbids, or ought not to do what the state commands. The state is to override conscience. Some may think that what we have in the end, then, in such cases, is in fact an assertion of the state's right to unreflective obedience. Some may think that claims of the ordinary kind about a right to obedience, despite what has been said, do issue in the indefensible assertion of a right to unreflective obedience.

Fortunately, this is confusion. We may indeed assert that the state may force a man to act, as we say, against his conscience. Sometimes doing so appears to raise moral questions and sometimes it does not. In no case, however, does doing so amount to the securing of unreflective obedience. To be unreflectively obedient is to act, more or less willingly, on the say-so of another. It is to give over one's conscience to another, by not thinking at all or by having one mistaken moral thought. It is *not* a matter of being *compelled* by another, or by the state, to act in a certain way. A man who is being compelled successfully to keep the law is being obedient, but not unreflectively obedient.

Indeed, one might say that if he *is* being compelled, it is logically impossible that he is being unreflectively obedient, since behaviour of the latter kind requires that he obey another *only*

because of the other's *command.* To assert that the state may often
force a man to act against his conscience, then, which may be the
upshot of certain arguments about authority, is *not* to assert that
the state ever has a right to unreflective obedience.

In summary of my entire discussion, then, there is a conceivable belief about a government's authority and hence a conceivable condemnation of a man who engages in political violence.
It is that he is failing in a particular obligation: to obey the law
for the reason, merely, that it has been made. Such a condemnation is deplorable, since it presupposes that the man should be
morally irresponsible. The argument against it, set out in three
parts above, is conclusive. However, it is entirely doubtful that
those who oppose violence have ever attempted the given condemnation. It would be mistaken, further, to suppose that this
condemnation of violence enters into other things. It is not
relevant to other contentions which mention a government's
authority. Its wrongfulness does not cast doubt on traditional
claims in political theory, and it does not put in question a belief
we have that a man may sometimes be forced by the state to go
against his conscience.

4. PRINCIPLES AND PROPOSITIONS

Let us make a fresh start, by considering a fundamental part
of Rawl's celebrated book, *A Theory of Justice.* In this part, or
these parts, it advances two basic principles for judging or
changing societies, and also a number of propositions about
political obligation. The argument for the principles is of the
same distinctive kind as the arguments for the propositions, and
has to do with the idea of a social contract.

However, the basic principles and the propositions about political obligation are connected by more than the fact that they
have similar supporting arguments. This is so, as may be guessed,
since any claim about political obligation in a society must have
a very great deal to do with the acceptability or unacceptability
of that society and hence with correct principles for judging
societies. It is hardly too much to say that one's political obligation *depends* on the goodness or badness of one's society.

Of course, the appraisal of societies comes into one's reflection on political violence where the special matter of political obligation is not in question. For example, there obviously are arguments against violence which do not have to do with obeying the law but do nonetheless have much to do with the state of societies. One can argue against violence, obviously, by citing the tolerable state of a society, and without mentioning the illegality of violence. Basic principles of judgement thus have a general importance. We shall pay a full attention both to the two which are offered here, and to the particular argument which is offered for them.

In what follows I shall expound in turn the argument having to do with a contract, the principles, and the propositions about political obligation, and then go on to objections and indeed to what I take to be a refutation. By way of anticipation, one of the two principles has to do with liberties and the other with the distribution of socio-economic goods. The propositions have to do with what is called a *natural duty* to obey the law and in general support one's society, and what is called an *obligation* to carry on in much the same way. Violence, given the duty and the obligation, is prohibited, or as good as prohibited.

To begin with what is presented as the fundamental part of the argument before us, we must engage in an activity of imagination. We imagine an assembly of people agreeing on the nature of their coming society. We do not engage in the speculation, rightly dismissed by Hume in his essay on the Social Contract, that they did once exist, or in the bizarre idea that we have inherited obligations from such actual founders of our own societies. We do not suppose, either, that our imagined people in their proceedings serve as a representation of some enterprise of agreement into which we ourselves enter tacitly by living in a society. None of these tedious or obscure things is in question. We merely conceive of people of a certain kind and in a certain situation agreeing on principles which will govern the society of which they are to be members.

It is of the first importance that our imagined people have particular characteristics and not others, and are in a particular situation. (i) They are *self-interested*. (ii) They are *equal* to one another in their freedom to advance conceptions and principles for consideration. (iii) They are also *rational*. That they are rational is no more than that they choose the best means to their ends, these ends being the possession of 'primary goods', and that they do not suffer from envy. Lastly, their situation is such that they know or believe certain things, but not others. (iv) They are said to have an awareness of general facts of human psychology, society, politics and economics. (v) It is essential that *none of them, however, knows anything of his own individual future in the society to come*. He does not know what his own natural assets and abilities will be, his economic and social place, even his own psychology or his conception of what is good. He thus does not know if he will be intelligent or otherwise, rich or poor, with or without prestige, and so on.

It is argued that our imagined assembly would agree on two principles as the basis of their coming society. They are principles of distribution, usually referred to in a somewhat question-begging way as principles of justice. Despite this good name, as we shall see, exception can be taken to them.

The first is that each member of a society is to have a right to the greatest amount of liberties which is consistent with each other member having the same. The liberties include political rights, freedom of expression, freedom of the person, and the right to hold private property. It is important that the first principle, named the Principle of Liberty, has priority over the second. That is, it is to be acted on first if both cannot be acted on together, and there are to be no departures from it at any stage of a society's development in the interest of a benefit in economic or social goods or their distribution. These latter things are the subject of the second principle. It, the Principle of Difference, specifies allowable socio-economic differences between classes in a society.

The first part of that principle is that 'social and economic inequalities are to be arranged so that they are. . .to the greatest benefit of the least advantaged. . . .'[6] What is intended appears to amount to two conditional propositions. The first is that *if* one class in a society is better off than others, this must somehow have the effect that the worst-off class in the society is better off than it would be without the inequality. This states a morally necessary

[6] *A Theory of Justice*, p. 302.

condition of an inequality, a necessary condition of the relative positions of the classes. It is a necessary condition of some people being well-off, relatively speaking, that those who are worst-off also benefit. The second proposition is that if a worst-off class is better off as an effect of another class's being in a better position, the latter class must remain in its fortunate position. This states a morally sufficient condition of the same inequality. It is a sufficient condition of some people being well-off that the worst-off also benefit.

By the first conditional proposition, then, to put the matter another way, we have it that the existence of a better-off class is *permissible* only if something else is true, and by the second proposition we have it that the existence of the better-off class is *obligatory* under the same condition.

As will be seen on reflection, the principle does not by itself tell one what equality or inequality a particular society should have. *No* inequality is allowable which does not improve the lot of the worst-off. Indeed, *if* a departure from a state of absolute *equality* in a particular society were not to make everyone better off, including a worst-off class which would then come into existence, the departure would not be acceptable. On the other hand, *any* inequality in a society is obligatory which *does* improve the lot of a worst-off class. It is therefore a logical possibility that the principle be satisfied in a society of no social and economic inequality whatever, in a society of overwhelming inequality, or in any society in between. The principle leads to a particular society only when it is conjoined with certain special propositions about individuals and their behaviour, resources and so on.

The particular propositions which are assumed in the doctrine before us, and lie behind the Difference Principle, are to the effect that some inequality will indeed be required in any society if all of its members, including some who have a lesser amount of social and economic goods, are to be as well off as they can be. Any alternative, a system with less or no inequality, will result in everyone, including the individuals just mentioned, being worse off. All this depends on the familiar reasoning that favourable inequalities are *incentives* which are necessary for a higher production of goods.

The Principle of Difference, as I have said, has two parts, of

which we now have one before us. In its second part, it is to
the effect that all members of the society are to have a considerable
and equal opportunity to gain any allowable positions of favourable inequality. This is not an afterthought, of secondary importance. On the contrary, this second part of the second principle
has priority over its first part. The society will not improve the lot
of a worst-off class if this can be done only by giving some
members an unequal opportunity to secure positions of favourable economic and social inequality.

As for priority generally, then, the Principle of Liberty ranks
first. Traditional rights, such as the right to vote, come before
progress toward equal opportunity and the reduction of poverty.
The second part of the Principle of Difference ranks second.
Equal opportunity to become as rich as is permitted, for example,
comes before the reduction of the poverty of a worst-off class.
The first part of the Difference Principle, having to do with a
worst-off class, ranks last.

As I have said, it is argued that our imagined assembly would
agree on the two principles and also their priority or ranking,
which is evidently of fundamental importance. Let us call this the
basic proposition of the doctrine before us. It *appears* to be basic,
certainly, and it is certainly so regarded by Rawls. It is, again,
that the imagined people, people in what is sometimes called *the
Original Position*, having the qualities they have and in their
prescribed ignorance and belief, would in fact choose the principles and their ranking.

The basic proposition is thought to enter essentially into an
argument for the rightness of the two principles, the two principles
as ranked, which is always to be understood. It is not that this
proposition, that the members of the imagined assembly would
agree on the principles, is taken to support the conclusion that
these would be the correct principles for *their* coming society,
which society we can also imagine. The basic proposition is
thought to be part of an argument for the moral superiority of
the principles for actual societies.[7] *Our* own societies are accept-

---

[7] *Op. cit.*, p. 17, p. 21, p. 42, p. 167, pp. 577–87. The basic
proposition is also thought to have two other uses, which I do not
consider here. See my article, 'The Use of the Basic Proposition of
a Theory of Justice', *Mind*, 1975.

able to the extent that they are informed by these principles rather than others, and this is a conclusion thought to be supported by the basic proposition. More precisely, the two principles are morally superior within the class of principles which have to do with the amount and distribution of goods. The two principles provide the correct answer to what is named the question of distribution or justice. A society governed by the two principles will be a society in which political violence will be unjustified.

The other part of the argument for the two principles is that the situation in which they allegedly would be chosen, the Original Position, would be a *fair* one.[8] The conditions under which an agreement on the principles would be reached in the imagined assembly would be fair to all. That is to say or to make the evaluation that no one would be under any disadvantage, or, more explicitly, under any wrongful disadvantage. What is important, and likely to be overlooked, is not that none of them has any disadvantage, where that is to talk simply of matters of fact, but that *none of them has any disadvantage of which we disapprove*. A horse-race illustrates the distinction. None of the horses is at a disadvantage, in the sense of wrongful disadvantage, because some of the horses carry more weight and thus, factually speaking, have a disadvantage.

What is important to the argument is that it is the conditions or the circumstance that would be fair, as distinct from the principles chosen, of which the same might be said. The conditions in question are of course those already mentioned, including the ignorance of the members of the imagined assembly as to their individual futures. The conditions secure that members of the assembly would be prevented from discriminating against any group in the society to come.

The whole argument before us, then, is taken to be this:

(i) the proposition that a certain choosing-circumstance would be a fair one,
(ii) the basic proposition, that people in that circumstance would choose the two principles, and
(iii) the conclusion that the two principles are justified.

[8] *Op. cit.*, p. 12, p. 120, Cf. p. 15, p. 18, p. 120, p. 121, p. 521.

The conclusion, more fully, is that the ordered principles of Liberty and Difference are those by which we are to assess our own societies. To the extent that these basic principles are realized in it, a society is a morally acceptable one. To the extent that a society is not in accord with the principles, it is not morally acceptable. We shall return to the two principles, and to the given argument for them, after we have before us the related propositions about political obligation.

Any proposition about political obligation, as we have already noticed, depends essentially on the state of society. We might then have in mind, in thinking of political obligation, an imagined society which is *fully in accord* with the two principles we have been considering. This might be of use in developing a theory. We might instead have in mind a society, to describe it quite insufficiently, which *comes near* to realizing the two principles. We might rather have in mind, as in fact we shall, our own societies. It is part of the doctrine we are considering that they have gone some considerable way toward realizing the two principles. In speaking of our societies, I mean such as the societies of Britain and America.[9]

The first proposition is that we, the members of these societies, have a *natural duty*. To express the proposition differently, we ought all to accept that we have a certain natural duty. It has two parts. The first is that we are to comply with, and do our share in, the just or nearly just institutions which are thought already to exist on our societies. A just institution, by specific definition, is one which is in accord with the two principles.

That the institutions are just or nearly just is not the argument for the duty. Of course, that the institutions are just or nearly so could naturally be taken on its own as a reason for political obligation. If a society is a good one, then as a matter of logic there is a duty to conform to it and support it, which will principally be a matter of conforming to its law. However, as we shall see in a moment, this reason for political obligation is in fact not the argument which is presented.

The natural duty, in its second part, is to assist in the establish-

[9] Rawls has in mind different things in different places. In 'The Justification of Civil Disobedience', *op. cit.*, he appears to be dealing with actual societies.

ing of new arrangements, just or more just, in areas in one's society where they do not yet exist. It is to be noted that the duty, in both its parts, does not derive in any way from our own voluntary acts. It is partly derived, as I have said, from the nature of one's society, but not at all from any act, say of promising or of taking benefit, which one has performed.

It will be clear that we do not have a precise account of this duty. In particular, we do not have a precise understanding of its weight. However, we are certainly to understand that the duty is a very considerable one. Certainly it is to be taken as ruling out acts of political violence. It is a part of our duty not to engage in violence, since we must comply with just institutions and it is accepted as part of the doctrine before us that our institutions of law are tolerably just. Indeed, it appears to be accepted in the doctrine that most or almost all of the institutions of our societies are either just or else decently on the way to it. Their being just, to repeat, is for them to be in accord with the two principles.

To come on to the argument for the natural duty, it is made to depend in part on this proposition: that it would be agreed by an imagined assembly of persons, somewhat different from before, that the members of societies like ours ought to have this duty. Those in the assembly, we suppose, are contemplating the possibility of being members of a society like ours. Hence, they have rather more general knowledge of their future society than those people choosing basic principles whom we imagined a few moments ago.[10] However, our present assembly is in other respects like the first one. The people in it are self-interested, equal, rational, and quite ignorant of what particular position each will have in the society to come. These things make for fairness.

Hence the whole of the argument for our natural duty, as will be expected, is as follows: a certain imaginable assembly would agree on such a duty for the members of societies like ours, more or less just societies, and this would be an agreement made in a fair situation, or under conditions of fairness. The argument, then, is analogous to the one for the two principles. It is pretty clear, incidentally, that an assembly would agree on the duty if, as we may suppose, it would earlier have agreed on the two principles,

[10] See above, pp. 61–62.

although under conditions of somewhat greater ignorance, and if our societies are taken to be decently on the way to implementing the two principles.

The second proposition to be considered is that we have a certain *obligation,* which is something distinct from the natural duty, to behave in certain ways. Suppose that by our voluntary actions we have gained benefits from an institution in our society, and furthermore, that the institution is a just or nearly just one. Under these conditions we have an obligation to support or to play a part in the institution in question. Thus we have both a natural duty and an obligation to support certain institutions. It appears that the institution of law counts as one of these. We have an obligation, then, as well as a duty, not to engage in political violence.

The whole argument for our having this obligation is of the same kind again. It is in part that the imagined assembly, contemplating membership in a society like ours, would agree on the obligation. In its other part the argument is that this would be an agreement made in a fair situation, one where no one was under a wrongful disadvantage.

5. THE ARGUMENTS REDUCED

The first of my objections, which will take a bit of time to lay out, has to do with the family of arguments. What I shall have to say pertains to all of them but I shall speak mainly of the first one, for the two principles of justice. It is, if repetition is bearable, (i) that a certain choosing-circumstance would be a fair one, (ii) that people in that circumstance would choose the two principles, and therefore (iii) that the principles are to be accepted.

This argument consists of an evaluative or normative premise and a factual premise. It is, then, of a familiar kind. The evaluative premise, that a certain situation of choosing would be a fair one, however much we may be inclined to accept it, is in a certain sense unsupported.[11] No proof of it is offered. We thus have an argument of precisely the kind that has led many philosophers

[11] For a relevant discussion by Rawls, but not one which materially affects the point see *A Theory of Justice,* pp. 577–87.

and others to say that the evaluative conclusions which are drawn are *without* 'justification'. Hence, what might be called the first and traditional enterprise of moral philosophy, to attempt to find firm foundations, is in no way advanced by the argument which includes the basic proposition. These are conclusions about the argument for the two principles as we are given it, and as I have just sketched it. In what follows I shall give a more explicit statement of the argument. As will be apparent, the same judgements can be made on the more explicit argument.

Perhaps, however, no justification of the kind traditionally pursued is possible. It may be that in reflection of this kind we have only lesser possibilities, one of which is to begin with the plain assertion of an unproved evaluative premise. It may even be that this is no worse than beginning from unquestioned 'axioms' in other kinds of inquiry. Let us take up this point of view, which cannot be confident but is hardly unreasonable, without further discussion. That is, let us agree to have some evaluative premise or other whose credentials are simply taken to be acceptable.

Both the evaluative and the factual premise get their detail or indeed their identity from the specification of the imagined assembly. It is necessary, at this point, to recall its features. It is (a) an assembly in which each person can and does pursue his own interest. (b) Each person has an equal ability and opportunity to do this. (c) Each makes a rational or effective choice, one which does in fact serve his ends and does not proceed from envy. The latter, envy, is taken to be a willingness to have one's own position worsened in order to worsen the position of another person who is better off. (d) Each is ignorant of any natural capabilities or attributes he will have in the society to come, his attitudes and moral outlook, his wealth or poverty, his social position. He does not know his future race, colour, religion, politics, culture, income or social standing. On the other hand, (e) each person has general beliefs about human psychology and about society, politics and economics. These beliefs are in fact regarded as being true, as being knowledge. It becomes apparent that they are principally beliefs about the paramount importance of liberty in societies and, it seems, the necessity of inequality to general well-being. The latter belief, implied by the Difference Principle, has to do with the familar doctrine about an incentive system.

The evaluative premise, then, is that an assembly of people satisfying all these conditions, (a) to (e), would constitute a fair choosing-situation, one involving no wrongful disadvantage. However, to come now to a first principal point, it is entirely clear that our acceptance of this premise, assuming that we do accept it, does not come out of thin air. What it comes out of are some moral convictions and some beliefs which we have. As seems plain from a number of passages, Rawls is aware of this fact if he does not state it so plainly or give it the prominence or repetition which he accords to other facts of the theory.[12]

What are the convictions and beliefs? There can be no mystery about that. They are convictions and beliefs which are given expression or effect by the conditions (a) to (e) mentioned above. We have the conviction (A) that each member of a society, each member of an actual society, has a right to goods, a rightful claim to what is in his interest. We accept (B) that each member has an equal right to such goods, or, at any rate, that we must pay attention to considerations of equality. We accept (C) that steps must be taken to realize each member's right, but that a man should not be worse off simply in order to reduce the benefits of someone else. We accept (D) that the rights in question do not depend on certain things, which are to be regarded as irrelevant. These will include race, colour, religion and so on. That is, we have convictions that certain facts about members of our societies ought to be irrelevant, and these are precisely such facts as those about their futures which the members of the imagined assembly are denied.

If our acceptance that the imagined situation would be fair must come out of these convictions, there is also something else from which it derives. We think, presumably, that the entire speculation is in another way acceptable. A fair choosing-situation, obviously, is one in which the people in question are not misled and do not have false beliefs. They are not disadvantaged in that way. Our acceptance of the imagined situation as fair, then, to put the matter briskly, must derive from (E) beliefs which *we* have about the important place of liberty in societies and also, presumably, about incentive systems.

[12] *Op. cit.*, pp. 14–21, p. 587.

It is the work of a moment, I think, to put to rest any doubt about the claim that our acceptance of the imagined choosing-situation as fair, assuming we do accept it, does depend on the given convictions and beliefs. Suppose that we did believe some benighted proposition contrary to (A). That is, suppose we believed that some members of societies, somehow identified, do not have any right to goods. If we did believe this, we would *not* approve as fair a choosing-situation of such a kind that it gave rise to a society where every member had such a right. Suppose that we believed, contrary to (D), that a man should be paid more simply because he is white-skinned. Suppose that we believed, contrary to (E), that it is just mistaken to give more importance to traditional liberties than to the reduction of poverty. We would then not approve of a choosing-situation which, in a word, does not reflect these beliefs. We would not regard it as a fair one.

The upshot is that the argument we are considering, to make it explicit, consists in:

(i) some moral convictions and some beliefs, which lead us to accept

(ii) that a certain imagined situation for choosing principles would be fair,

(iii) the basic supposition that people in such a situation would choose two principles, and

(iv) the conclusion that the principles have a recommendation.

We can call this the *Contract Argument* for the principles.

Some may be inclined to think, at first thought, that the first premise is not logically distinct from the second. The truth is otherwise. One part of the second premise, about fairness, is to the effect that a choosing-situation in which people could not allow the colour of a man's skin to determine his liberties would be in that respect fair. This is evidently distinct from the conviction that a man's skin-colour ought to be irrelevant to his liberties.

Some may think, secondly, that to set out the argument in the four steps is to set it out uneconomically. They may feel that it can be set out more efficiently as it was before, consisting just in the assertion that a certain choosing-situation would be a fair one,

F

the assertion that people in that situation would choose the two principles, and the conclusion that the principles have a recommendation.

Several things might be pointed out about this. The most important is that what appears in the first part of the four-part argument must in fact occur in any expression of the argument which is complete. It is plain enough where it does occur in the three-part argument. It occurs in the initial premise, that a certain choosing-situation would be a fair one, one in which no one is at a wrongful disadvantage. To assert this premise, plainly, is partly to assert that the choosing-situation is in accord with certain convictions. The situation, for example, is in accord with the conviction that skin-colour ought to be irrelevant to certain things.

In what follows, then, let us have in mind the four-part form of the Contract Argument. What is to be said for this form, in general, is simply that it is fully explicit. All that I shall have to say of the argument in this form, evidently, will be relevant to other forms of it.

Let us put all this aside for a moment and consider a different and common kind of reflection on societies and principles. Suppose one wishes to arrive at principles for the governance of one's actual society. One wishes, that is, to get an answer to the question of distribution or justice. One begins with one's convictions and beliefs. They are to the effect that each member of a society is to be regarded as having a right to goods of one kind and another, and that steps are to be taken to secure this right. As it happens, one's convictions and beliefs are precisely those sketched a little way back, (A) to (E). *Having got them straight, one advances directly to the conclusion that the best answer to the question of justice amounts to the two principles of justice of which we know.* The principles, of course, as in the case of the Contract Argument, are in good part no more than generalizations or summations or adjustments of the convictions, although there is much more that might be said. What one will have done is produce what we shall call an *Ordinary Argument* for the two principles.

The first thing that I wish to urge about the two arguments is that the Ordinary Argument is *as good* as the Contract Argument in giving support to the two principles. From what has been said so far, of course, it is less than clear that either argument is much good. There is an impressive gap, or rather, nothing so clear as a gap, between the premise or the premise-set and the shared conclusion. It is arguable, of course, that many principles could not get support from either the premise of the Ordinary Argument or the set of premises in the Contract Argument. Racist principles, and principles of discrimination generally, are in this group. However, there are more left over than only the Principles of Liberty and Difference.

Can the Contract Argument be improved? In *A Theory of Justice* a good deal of effort is put into arguing for the truth of the basic proposition: that the assembly would choose the two principles. The argument, in one important part, is that each member of the assembly, in comparing different principles or groups of principles, would realize that all of them, save total equality, would have within them the possibility of different upshots for the member in his future life in the society. He might be among the rich or among the poor, for example, and he cannot know in advance. He would, it is suggested, be of such attitudes as to *maximin*: that is, to choose the particular conception whose worst possible upshot for him would be more acceptable than the worst possible upshots of other conceptions. Each member of the assembly would, as a result, be led to favour the Principle of Difference. What this amounts to is in fact a further characterization of the assembly.

There is another essential matter to be kept in mind if we proceed in this way. We must also suppose, to keep the whole doctrine standing, that the enlarged conception *persists* as a conception of a *fair* choosing-situation. *We* must then have certain convictions or beliefs. We must, in short, have a commitment to the maximin principle.

I have suggested that at first sight, or in its first presentation, the Contract Argument is no better than the Ordinary Argument in producing the two principles of justice as conclusion. We now suppose, however, that the Contract Argument can be strengthened. This is done by characterizing the imagined assembly more fully and adding the feature just mentioned. If the Contract Argument can be strengthened in this way, however, to come to to the main point here, it is necessarily true that the Ordinary Argument can be strengthened to the same extent. One adds one's strengthening conviction to the premise of the Ordinary Argument. One adds the conviction that one should always choose the policy whose worst upshot will be best. In general, *whatever* is done to the Contract Argument can have a counterpart with respect to the Ordinary Argument. The latter will be as good, bad or indifferent as the former.[13]

What follows from this, I take it, is the conclusion that the *actual grounds* implicit in the Contract Argument, however adumbrated, are identical with the grounds in some version of the Ordinary Argument. *All* that actually gives support to the conclusion in the Contract Argument is the first premise, a certain collection of convictions and beliefs. All that actually gives support to the conclusion is exactly and no more than that which supports the conclusion in the Ordinary Argument. *What we have called the basic proposition in the Contract Argument is logically irrelevant to it. So too is the evaluative proposition that the imagined choosing-situation would be a fair one.* The Contract Argument is the Ordinary Argument with two superfluous parts. What is taken to be the foundation of the Contract Argument is in fact no part of the structure. Reflection on the basic proposition, so-called, let alone prolonged reflection, is idle. So too for the proposition about fairness.

(The analogy is incomplete and maybe a bit unfair, but one is put in mind of the sociologist, say, who comes to some conclusion about the nature of society. He does so only on the basis of certain *evidence* and by way of certain *canons of inquiry*. He proceeds to attribute belief in precisely his evidence as well as acceptance of precisely his canons of inquiry to an imagined conference of sociologists. He is pleased to discover that the conference would confirm his conclusion. From the point of view of the logic of the situation, the validity of the argument, the imagined conference is an irrelevancy.

---

[13] I have left out, incidentally, some formal conditions on principles that might be taken to be part of the first premise of the Contract Argument, and also some practical considerations. Both can evidently also go into the Ordinary Argument. *Op. cit.*, p. 46, p. 175.

The analogy between the assembly and the sociological conference, incidentally, becomes nearer to complete if we make our sociologist a bit odder still. He imagines a conference of sociologists who do not in fact have precisely his evidence and canons, but, for some reason, draw a conclusion *as if they had*. What leads me to say this, of course, is that the members of the assembly have no moral convictions, but, for reasons we know, they behave as they would if they did have.)

It is worth noticing, in partial explanation of the error of thinking that the basic proposition does have some logical utility, that something like it does have utility when it turns up in other speculations about a Social Contract, those traditional ones mentioned some way back in this essay and having to do with actual people and the grounds of political obligation. Suppose that somehow *we* do tacitly *commit ourselves* to our societies and their principles. We may, then and afterwards, have convictions that lead us to think the principles are good ones. Thus there is that reason for going along with them. However, our observance of the principles also has this to be said for it: we promised it. This proposition, one that is related to the basic proposition in the doctrine we are considering, provides an independent argument of some strength or other for our observance. At any rate the proposition would do so if it were true.

I should like to anticipate one objection to what has been claimed. The people in the imagined assembly, we have granted, would *agree* on the principles. The objection, which will barely survive being made explicit, is that some recommendation attaches to the principles simply because they would be *agreed upon* by the people.

What recommendation is it? We must not drift into thinking, obviously, that any real person has ever made such an agreement and so acquired an obligation. The Social Contract, in its traditional form, is dead and buried. It remains so if we grant, as we are urged, that '*we*' *would* agree to the principles *if* we were as the people in the Original Position are.[14] *We* are different, have never been there, and have made no agreement.

If we stick firmly to the supposition, that imagined people would agree on the principles, there is still no recommendation

[14] *Op. cit.*, p. 13.

in the bare fact of their agreement. Suppose we imagine an assembly made up of people who know that the coming society will have in it weak and powerful members. Moreover, and more important, each person in the assembly knows where he will turn up, whether he will be weak or powerful. Suppose, then, that the assembly comes to agree on principles which will favour those who will be powerful, and that this comes about essentially as a result of an awareness of that future state of affairs. We will not suppose, I think, that the fact that there would be this agreement would recommend the principles. The mere fact of agreement in an imagined assembly is by itself of no relevance to us. If, incidentally, the example just imagined is taken not to be one of satisfactory or full agreement, but rather an example involving something like coercion, it is easy enough to think of an alternative. There is the assembly with false beliefs, to mention but one.

What confers relevance, if no more, on an imagined agreement, are the conditions under which it is made. The recommendation of the agreed principles, in that case, rests on the conditions, and on the convictions that support them. What we have in the Contract Agreement as sketched, with no reliance placed on the bare fact of agreement.

In any case, talk of agreement in the imagined assembly, like talk of *an assembly* at all, is quite otiose for a reason so far unmentioned. What we are contemplating, if we are following the instructions, is an assembly of *identical persons*. At any rate we contemplate them only insofar as they are identical. Each is taken only to have precisely the qualities that have been mentioned. If we set about assigning them other qualities, perhaps various and compensating knowledges of capabilities of judgement, we depart from our instructions. It is not suggested that we are to do this, and if we attempt it, the truth of the basic proposition becomes still more uncertain than it is if we follow our instructions. What we do, then, in short, is imagine identical persons. In this case, all talk of *agreement* is otiose or pointless. We might as well have imagined *a single individual* and not an assembly.[15] For this reason alone, an elabor-

[15] Rawls, in passing and perhaps implicitly, grants the point. *Op. cit.*, p. 139.

ated theory of the kind we are considering verges on the ridiculous.[16]

So much for the structure of the Contract Argument for the two principles. Perhaps, in the confines of this essay, I have attended too much to the structure of the argument. Still, the doctrine about political obligation we are considering is given by its author as all of a piece, a piece in which the Contract Argument is fundamental. Also, there is the matter already noticed, having to do with The Impressive in political philosophy. It is worth remarking, in this connection, that it is not as if the structure of the argument were something in every way distinct from the force of the argument, the final worth. Strictly speaking, of course, the final worth of the argument is not affected by the discovery that it has redundant parts, parts on which the conclusion does not depend. Nonetheless many people are likely to think more of the Contract Argument when it is presented to them than they would think of the Ordinary Argument. The structure itself distracts attention from the prime question of whether the two principles are an adequate generalization and reconciliation of the collection of attitudes and beliefs. One is less likely to see how much a matter of hesitant judgement it must be, rather than a matter of anything like plain logical fact, that the two principles follow as a conclusion from what goes before. One is less likely to see, too, how hesitant one's judgement must be about supposed consequences of the principles, notably those having to do with violence.

To persist with structure for a moment more, there are also the given arguments for the two propositions about political obligation. Again, what is taken to be fundamental appears to me to be logically irrelevant. There are certain special complexities here but let us pass them by. What I shall do is merely state, pretty roughly, the actual arguments which are contained in the presented arguments. These actual arguments are analagous, of course, to the Ordinary Argument.

(a) Given certain convictions and beliefs, the same as outlined

[16] A second objection to my fundamental criticism would have to do with a view of the Contract Argument as other than a plain matter of premises and conclusion. See p. 21, pp. 48–9, p. 579. One can, however, take the same view of the Ordinary Argument.

above for the Ordinary Argument, and given the belief that our societies are decently on the way toward achieving a goal defined by the two principles of justice, it follows that we have a natural duty to support and advance the institutions of our societies. In particular we must abide by the law and refrain from violence.

(b) Given the convictions and beliefs as before, and given that we have chosen to benefit from institutions in our societies which are in accord with the two principles, we have an obligation to play our part in the institutions. In particular, we are obliged to abide by the law and refrain from violence.

6. THE PRINCIPLES AGAIN

It seems plain enough that the Ordinary Argument does not come near to *establishing* the two principles in their ordering as the basic principles for the judging and directing of societies. It follows, given what has been said, and perhaps it is evident any-way, that the same is true of the Contract Argument. It may be, further, that nothing so neat and ordered as is suggested by the word 'argument', as usually used, will ever convince one that any basic principles are the right ones. Also, a ramified thing which is larger and looser than an argument, if it does produce a kind of conviction about particular principles, is unlikely to 'establish' them, let alone 'demonstrate' them. It is unrealistic to hope for the neat cogency which the words suggest.

It must be allowed, of course, despite the weakness of the Ordinary Argument and the Contract Argument, that their sup-posed conclusion is nonetheless correct. That is, it might be that the two principles are indeed the right principles for society. Are they? The question is obviously too large to be settled finally here. Something needs to be said, however, partly because of the relation of the two principles to the propositions about duty and obligation, propositions on which we also need to come to some judgement. They also may be better, so to speak, than the given argument for them.

The two principles are mainly compared by Rawls with the Principle of Utility. The latter principle is taken to be the most important alternative, and much argument against it is offered.

The argument in the end is quite familiar: the Principle of Utility countenances inequality or unfairness, indeed calls for it, when this happens to maximize the total of satisfaction. The two principles may be regarded as superior to the Principle of Utility in that they make a place for equality. The first principle calls for *equal* liberty and the second puts a restraint on inequalities. Of course, while we do in fact accept the familiar argument against the Principle of Utility, and hence cannot be Utilitarians, we share what might be called the basic attitude which moved Bentham and Mill in their reflections. That is, we are in favour of reducing distress and increasing satisfaction. This attitude also enters into the two principles of justice. The first principle calls for a certain *maximum* of liberty, the possession of liberty being a source of satisfaction and its lack a matter of distress. The second principle specifies that *less* distress or *more* satisfaction for a worst-off group may be purchased at the cost of inequalities.

To grant that the two principles are superior to the Principle of Utility, however, is not to grant all that much. There are other principles which also are superior to Utility. These also have the virtue of giving a place to equality. One will be suggested by certain criticisms that can be made of the two principles.

(i) By the first principle, that of Liberty, a society is to accord to its members the maximum amount of liberties consistent with all members having the same amount. This principle takes precedence over the second one, the Principle of Difference. Let us consider this precedence, if briefly. It is, in part, that there is to be no infringement of a man's or a group's liberties even if this will serve to raise the socio-economic level of the worst-off class in society. There is this prohibition on interference with liberties at any stage of social progress.

It is not made absolutely clear what we are to have in mind as the liberties in question. This failure makes discussion disagreeable, but not impossible. If a rough description is worthwhile, let us think of those things, including various property-rights, which are commonly mentioned as liberties in our societies. Surely it cannot be acceptable that there should be an absolute prohibition on interference with these things. It is not too much to say that social progress in the past, now approved by all, has *depended* on infringements of such things. Can it be thought that no possible future advancement will be worth an infringement? Is it certain that the present amount of liberties had by each member of our societies is correct? With less of certain liberties, presumably, there would be less socio-economic inequality.

There is also an objection which has to do with the fact that the liberties are merely rights in a certain standard sense. That is, to have a liberty is not necessarily to have the power to act on it. My right to hold property does not ensure that I own anything whatever. Should there not be equality in powers? Rawls has something to say of the question but hardly enough.

My main criticism here, however, which will not be developed further, is the other one. The place which should be given to *some* principle about liberties is not the large place given the Principle of Liberty in the doctrine before us.

(ii)   As we have noticed, the Principle of Difference is a re- sponse to what we may call the Utilitarian and the Equalitarian attitudes. The principle recommends itself to us, in part, because it is for the reduction of distress and then the increase of satisfac- tion. To have this, we are to pay a price, which is the acceptance of an allegedly necessary amount of inequality. The principle recommends itself to us, in part, because it is against inequality. It is against all inequality save that amount just mentioned.

Nonetheless, the Difference Principle appears to be in a way inferior to something else, another principle for socio-economic affairs, which also expresses the Utilitarian and the Equalitarian attitudes.

Let us approach it by freely imagining stages in the develop- ment of a society, a society which is in fact governed in its socio- economic affairs by the Principle of Difference. (1) In an initial stage, there is some socio-economic inequality and the worst-off class is in great distress. The facts of this society, which partly have to do with human motivation and the need for incentives, are such that an increase in inequality will benefit the worst-off class. Hence, (2) since the society is governed by the Difference Principle, it comes to have more inequality than before, but with the worst-off class now in a lesser distress. However, it becomes clear that the new inequality which actually comes to exist is greater than is needed to sustain the worst-off class in its con- dition. Hence (3) through a transfer of goods, the society comes to have less inequality and a worst-off class not in distress at all. It is, of course, less satisfied than the other classes of the society. (4) Then, through fundamental changes of several kinds, including changes in the kind of incentives which are necessary, the society comes to a state such that all of its members are *well-satisfied*, and also *equally satisfied*. We may suppose that the level of satisfaction is very high indeed, and end our speculation about the society's progress at this point.

However, it is to be noticed that there will be a further change required by the Difference Principle if a certain condition comes to be satisfied. That is, there must be a reintroduction of inequality if for some reason this will make even the least-satisfied class which thus comes into existence better off than the society as a whole in the fourth stage. And obviously that is not necessarily the end. That it is not the end seems to me important.

Before we consider this, there is a point to be noticed about the fourth stage. We have supposed that what happens there, like the rest of the imagined sequence, is in accord with the Difference Principle. Is this so? Does the principle call for the mentioned fundamental changes which make the fourth stage possible? Does the principle enjoin the society to educate or somehow change its members away from demanding certain rewards for contributing to the well-being of the less able? It is not clear, but one can reasonably suppose so. The principle allows only those rewards or favourable inequalities which are *necessary* to the given end. It may be argued that a certain kind of level of reward is not necessary since a change in the demanding attitudes of individuals is possible, and such a change would allow the end to be achieved by way of different or less reward, and hence less inequality. Let us then take it that the Difference Principle does enjoin a society to reduce or change the incentives required for the given end, and hence that the fourth stage is in accord with the principle. If the principle does not enjoin this, it is open to objection.

Is our inclination to support the Difference Principle explained by the fact that what it recommends to us is a certain progression, one exemplified by our imagined society's four stages *and* the further ones? That is, is our support for the Difference Principle explained by its recommending to us, as it does, a progression which in a certain sense has no end? I do not think so. We are inclined to support the Difference Principle because it brings to mind the progression culminating in a situation exemplified by the *fourth stage* of the imagined society. Although it is difficult to be sure about the reasons, it does seem likely that it is the fact that it makes for progress toward *equal well-being* which really recommends the Difference Principle.

Given this proposition, there is reason to favour a socioeconomic principle other than the Difference Principle. There is at least reason to *add* a further socio-economic principle, and to give it a kind of precedence over the other. The new principle, unlike the Difference Principle, gives relatively precise expression to our commitment to the fourth stage. The Principle of Equal Socio-Economic Satisfaction, as we may call it, is to the effect that the policies of a society are to make for progress toward all of its members being equally well-satisfied.

It can be said, of course, that this principle would not carry us so far as the Difference Principle. That is, it would not give us any further guidance if we reached the stage of equal satisfaction, somehow defined. It does not rule out further change as desirable, but it does not specify that change either. This is so. However, since the need for the further guidance is so remote, and since anyway we do not have to give up the Difference Principle entirely, we need not be troubled.

Some may suppose that my suggestion of a different or a further principle is pedantic. After all, the Difference Principle does have the consequence which is specified in the principle about equal well-being. It can reasonably be replied, I think, that there is a good deal to be said for a kind of accuracy in the expression of our inclinations. Indeed, although the subject is large and difficult, it is not obvious that we should want to carry on beyond the fourth stage, somehow defined, if we reached it.

There is also another reply. We are agreed, let us suppose, that we want to reach the fourth stage, whatever we would want thereafter. We are agreed too, given our actual societies, that the fourth stage is more important *to us* than anything that might come after. We have two possible principles of guidance, each of which can take us to the fourth stage. It seems, however, that they differ in what can be called *effectiveness*. That is, they differ in the extent to which they are likely to give rise to action. What I have in mind is partly that the Difference Principle sets us upon an endless road, and that travellers on such roads drag their feet.

There is a larger point about effectiveness. The Difference Principle is that a society can and should have the inequalities, if only the inequalities, which make the position of the worst-off better than it would otherwise be. Thus another difference between it and the principle of equal satisfaction is that it might reasonably be called defeatist and can undoubtedly be called cautious. Although it partly derives from a commitment to equality, it is so expressed as to bring into great prominence the admittedly consistent demand for incentive-inequalities. The analogy, for various reasons, is a loose one, but it is as if the Utilitarians, instead of urging us to maximize total satisfaction, had urged us to pursue the distress, but only the distress, that will serve to maximize satisfaction in the end.

It will be said, of course, that caution about equality is required, and that it is a good thing to give it expression in the formulation of the principle. A single sentence cannot end this particular dispute, but it is worth noting that socio-economic history shows no shortage of claims as to the necessity of various inequalities, claims which have long since been falsified.

There is a related point. There is in fact hardly a more established controversy in economic thinking than that one between those who believe in the necessity of much inequality as a means to an end, and those who believe that much less inequality would suffice as a means to the end. On the other hand, there can be little doubt that we should pursue an ideal of equality. If we have an area of agreement, or something like it, and an area of controversy, it is as well to separate them. The Principle of Difference brings together what is best kept apart.

Neither of these objections, (i) or (ii), to the Principles of Liberty and Difference and their ordering, has been argued for sufficiently. What can be claimed, perhaps, is that enough has been said to raise appreciable doubts. It would in my view be mistaken to take the second objection less seriously because it is an objection to what can be called the style rather than the substance of the Difference Principle. Fundamental principles are propositions of a certain character. The same thought, in a certain sense, can obviously have different attitudinal embodiments.

What one has in a principle is a function not only of what in some restricted sense it states, but also of how it states it, a function not only of what it states but also of its informing spirit. It is important that what is stated by a principle reflects our convictions, but it is quite as important that its spirit does so.

7. THE DUTY AND THE OBLIGATION

The Contract Argument for the two principles reduces to the Ordinary Argument, and the subsequent arguments about political obligation and hence violence reduce to analogues of the Ordinary Argument. The first of these in one formulation is that given certain convictions and beliefs, and given that our societies are decently on the way to realizing the two principles, it follows that we have a natural duty to support and advance the institutions of our societies. We have a natural duty to obey the law and to refrain from violence.

We may suppose that the conclusion follows from the premises, but, as what has been said already clearly suggests, the premises are open to question. The collection of convictions and beliefs is in part at least controversial. For example, there is the belief that certain liberties have an importance greater than anything else. This point was to be anticipated, of course, since the same objection has been made to the summation of the convictions and beliefs in the two principles.

Furthermore, even if we accepted the convictions and beliefs and the two principles without hesitation, there is the question of how far our societies do in fact realize them. Let us give some attention to this, or rather, to the limited question of whether our societies are decently on the way to realizing the Principle of Difference, which clearly is superior to many other socio-economic principles. That our societies *are* decently on the way is obviously essential to the argument about duty.

To speak particularly of Britain and America, are these societies tolerably well on the way to having only those inequalities which are necessary if a worst-off class is to be better off than otherwise it would be? The question is far from precise. Let us take it to be tantamount to something else, perhaps slightly better: Are these societies *so much* on the way to having only *necessary* inequalities that their members have a weighty duty, however 'natural' or 'unnatural', to obey the law? It is allowed, in the doctrine we are considering, that things may *seem* otherwise. That is, it is allowed that it may *seem* likely that there is an awful lot of unnecessary inequality. At this point, an additional economic consideration is introduced.[17]

It is that the production of goods depends not only on an incentive system, but on something that in our societies is closely connected with it, real capital accumulation. What we are to understand is that we could, for one or a few generations, reduce the gap between rich and poor, by reducing benefits to the rich, and that we would not pay the price of reducing the state of life of the poorest. However, this would have the effect of reducing real capital accumulation and hence, in the end, the effect of depriving future generations of the poorest of a certain degree of well-being that might otherwise have been theirs. I have stated the argument briefly but not, I hope, unfairly.

One reply, which seems obvious, is that there is but a contingent connection between real capital accumulation and the existence, as we know it, of extreme economic and social inequality. One can hardly ignore the fact that there exist different economies which satisfy an analogous requirement of real capital accumulation and do not do so by lodging the capital with a class of overwhelming privilege. There seems no quick or slow argument to the conclusion that a society *must* do its saving by sustaining the existence of great inequalities. We need not dismay ourselves by the reflection that the economic theory in question is extensive and unsettled. We can rest on the fact that there do exist economies which face futures as secure as those of America and Britain and do not sustain similar systems of inequality. There *are* economies, as satisfactory as ours, which are without the rich.

Two other things are to be said against the idea, which, it will be as well to say, appears to me a *wild* idea, that our societies are sufficiently far on the way to having only necessary inequality that members of them have a weighty political obligation. It is surely evident that there exists some such obligation, of course, somehow

[17] 'Distributive Justice', *op. cit.*, pp. 73–5.

grounded. What seems absolutely implausible is that it can be grounded on the proposition about necessary inequalities.

The first thing is that to think that we *are* decently on the way to having only necessary inequalities is very likely to be out of touch, for one reason or another, with the magnitude of existing inequalities. This is a matter, in part, of that ignorance of the facts of inequality noticed in the first essay in this book.

To approach the question of magnitude in one way, it is in no way rhetorical to observe that some large minority of members of our societies, if their lives were altered in a certain way, would experience them as lives of horror. I have in mind an alteration such that their new existence would be one which *is* in fact the lot of another minority. If we who are in the minority of privilege bring to mind, and not for a passing moment, what touches us most closely, perhaps our children and their situation, it must be impossible to think of tolerating the alteration. It includes those existing schools which make our commitment to equal opportunity no more than hypocrisy. They are schools which blight and constrict the entire lives of the children who go to them.

Shall we say that such an existence would carry a distress for us unlike the distress now caused to those who new experience it? No doubt this is in some degree true. Distress in part is a consequence of expectation. Destructive circumstances have a lesser effect on those who have not anticipated anything else. For such reasons there once was, whether in terms of equality or in terms of satisfaction and distress, *a* defence of the institution of slavery. Certainly neither the bare lack of such goods as freedom and property, nor inequality in these goods, is of fundamental importance. What is important is avoidance of the experience of distress, and it may be avoided despite the absence of certain goods. What is important is equality of experience, which might obtain despite inequality of goods.

Nonetheless, the argument of different expectations is a vanishing one. Each slave class took up, to an increasing extent, the expectations of its masters. Today, oppressed classes in our societies are aware of their situation to a very considerable degree. That their awareness is not yet ours does not make it reasonable to continue to weigh the goods of the world in two sets of scales. Inequality of experience in our societies is in fact great.

The other remark about necessary inequalities has already been made in another connection. It cannot be in dispute that virtually every major economic and social advance in history, every advance in the direction of equal well-being, has been resisted by an argument about supposedly necessary inequalities. Almost no one takes the view, now, that the inequalities *were* necessary to things of importance. No one takes the view that any losses suffered did outweigh the gains. We have here, to speak too quickly, an iron inductive argument for scepticism about all claims as to necessary inequalities in our present societies.

What remains is to draw a conclusion about the argument for our supposed natural duty to obey the law and hence to refrain from violence. It cannot be that we have no duty whatever. We have *more* of a duty than we would have in a slave society. It has not been shown, however, to state the proposition as best one can, that there is *a weighty duty*. Our circumstance is *far* from an imagined one which is also considered by Rawls, where the members of a society are members of an ideal society and so have a weighty and indeed an overwhelming duty to support it.

Let us leave the duty and pass on to the obligation which we are thought to have. Given the same convictions and beliefs as before, and given that we have voluntarily acted so as to benefit from institutions in our societies which are in accord with the two principles, we have an obligation to play our part in the institutions. What is to be said against this is partly the same as with the natural duty. The convictions and beliefs are not beyond question. The two principles are not beyond question. Hence even if the institutions of our societies are in accord with the principles, we do not have the simple fact that we have benefited from institutions which are clearly defensible.

We may reflect, however, that there is *something* to be said for, say, the Principle of Difference. Do we then have a resulting weighty obligation? The answer depends, as before, on whether institutions of our society do in fact come near enough to being in accord with the principle, and hence having only certain necessary inequalities. I have already suggested that there is not much reason for thinking so.

There are further difficulties about the obligation. It is not clear, despite what is said about voluntarily accepting benefits, how

G

the obligation is supposed to come into being. Suppose a man does accept a benefit by invoking the law in order to protect his own property, and then breaks a law for political reasons. In so doing he destroys the property of someone else. In what does the wrongfulness of his act consist? What is the particular wrongfulness which has to do with the fact that he has used the law in his own interest previously? Is it that a consideration of consistency or equality enters into the argument? That is, does the wrongfulness consist in treating like cases, cases of property-ownership, differently? One of the difficulties in the way of this line of argument is that the two cases, although alike when considered in terms of property-ownership, are fundamentally different. To say no more, one is a case of *political* violence.

Alternatively, if it is an alternative, does the wrongfulness of the political act consist in the fact that it is not an acceptance of rightful *debt*? This is suggested by the emphasis on voluntary action in connection with the obligation. Here we have it that by voluntarily benefiting from an institution of his society, the man acquires a certain debt. We can say that certain behaviour on his part is now owed, or called for, or fitting. This behaviour is precisely other than the behaviour of destroying the property of others.

There clearly are replies. First, if the man believed that a minority of his society was being degraded, he rightly might not allow himself to be restrained from violent political action by the single fact that he had been a beneficiary himself. Rather the contrary, perhaps. What is said in explanation and defence of the obligation leaves out of consideration all people other than the man himself and those individuals whose property he may destroy.

Again, assuming that the man does in fact acquire some debt by making use of the law in his own interest, how large is that debt? Could it be that if it exists at all it is very small indeed? Consider an opposite case. Most people would not feel that a man had gone any way toward justifying the setting of a bomb if he established that he had eschewed, as far as he could, the benefits offered to him by society. He would not do himself much good by pointing out that he had not called the police when his house was broken into. The smallness of his defence indicates the smallness of the accusation that can be made in our primary case, where a man is claimed to have disregarded the debt acquired by voluntarily acting in such a way as to benefit from society.

Our supposed obligation, then, seems a still smaller thing than our natural duty. There do exist strong arguments against political violence. If there is an argument at all which has to do with the supposed obligation, it is not among the strong arguments.

Let us finish by recalling the several main conclusions of this discussion of *A Theory of Justice*.

The Contract Argument for the Principles of Liberty and Difference as ordered, by which we are to judge our societies, contains parts thought to be basic but which in fact contribute nothing to the force of the argument. The same is true of the analogous arguments for our supposed natural duty and our obligation to obey the law, and hence to refrain from violence. There is a likelihood, in the case of each argument, that its expendable machinery will distract attention from its value. Its value is no greater than that of a related simpler argument.

If one looks at the two principles directly, or, much the same, looks at the convictions and beliefs which are their source, one finds several grounds for objection. One has to do with the place given to liberties, another with the character of the Principle of Difference.

Objection must also be made to the claims about natural duty and obligation. One large point here is that the arguments for the duty and the obligation, and hence for refraining from violence, presuppose that our societies are decently on the way to realizing the Principle of Difference. They are not.

3

On Democratic Violence

If we look at contemporary writing on political violence in the hope of finding cogent arguments, either for or against it, and if we are not too disposed to take a side, we are unlikely to be satisfied. This pessimism certainly does not derive only from the writings looked at in the first two essays of this book. In Sartre and Fanon, an impassioned commitment to the oppressed issues in the judgement that violence is not only permissible but obligatory. That some men are made less than men, that they have their stature taken from them, appears to be taken as an adequate ground for their violence, violence which is to change them. '. . .to shoot down a European,' we are told, 'is to kill two birds with one stone, to destroy an oppressor and the man he oppresses at the same time.'[1] It is not hard to find questions about the argument, even given an understanding and not merely an awareness of facts about colonial oppression and personality. Most of us, to pass on to but one other example, will be as reluctant to suppose that the 'historical calculus' offered to us by Marcuse can be shown to issue in the conclusion that political violence of the Left generally has a justification.[2] Can there be much more than metaphor in talk of the *rules* given us by history?

Some of course, will find scepticism about Sartre, Fanon and

[1] Jean-Paul Sartre, preface to Frantz Fanon, *The Wretched of the Earth*, trans. Constance Farrington, (London, 1965). A similar idea is at the centre of Georges Sorel's *Reflections on Violence*. For an enlightening account of Sorel's thought, see Isaiah Berlin's lecture printed in *The Times Literary Supplement*, No. 3,644, 31 December, 1971.

[2] Herbert Marcuse, 'Ethics and Revolution', *Revolution and the Rule of Law*, ed. Edward Kent (Englewood Cliffs, N. J., 1971).

Marcuse congenial, but not scepticism about others. It is, for me, difficult to see this as other than a result of being too disposed to take a side. To return for a moment to Rawls, we should be as reluctant to take up his equally resolute conclusions.[3] It really cannot be that it is economic *necessity* that principally explains the fact that our societies are only distant approximations of the society of justice. It cannot be that the intransigence of privileged classes is not a principal part of the explanation. If so, and it seems to me entirely beyond denial, we must at least question the prohibition on violence, based largely on the idea that our societies come about as close to justice as can be demanded.

It remains obscure what total of things would enter into really effective argumentation, which surely is possible, either for or against violence. Certainly some group of basic principles would be fundamental, as would the facts of inequality and the facts of violence. Presumably some complete assessment of claims about political obligation would have a place. There could be no avoiding judgements about reactions to violence, reactions justified or unjustified, on the part of the state, privileged classes, and others, and, more generally, there could be no avoiding judgements on the rationality of engaging in violence.

There is also something else, which cuts across some of these subjects. It will be valuable, and I suspect essential, in any effective argumentation, to consider how violence is related to other practices, relevant practices about which we have clearer judgements. One of these, perhaps the most important, is democracy.

Many of those who condemn violence do so on the ground that it is undemocratic. Many of its apologists are in some agreement with those who condemn it. Their endeavour is to find higher reasons for what they accept, implicitly or explicitly, to be undemocratic. My first purposes in this essay are to see clearly how political violence stands to the practice and the rules of democracy, and to the arguments for the practice and the rules. The latter relationship, between some violence and the arguments for democracy, will then enter into a characterization of one important type of political violence. In the end, we shall be further on the way to having an adequately reasoned conclusion about the morality of violence.

[3] See above, Essay 2, Parts 4–7.

1. DEMOCRACY

We must first recollect and perhaps become clearer about the nature of democracy, or rather democracy as best conceived in the last few decades of the tradition with which most of us are familiar. It is *a practice in which the people choose and then influence those who do govern the nation and direct its relations of war and peace.* This is but a rubric, and a rubric that might stand at the head of different texts. Even so, since we shall be concerned with such systems of government as those in Britain and America, it provides us with a conception which is more apposite than certain alternatives. I have in mind the alternative idea of government *by* the people, and the alternative idea of government whose covert function is the oppression of most of the people by an ascendant class.

We can clarify our conception of democracy by prising apart three groups of features, which also will serve as criteria for the assessment of existing systems. None of this will be amazingly novel stuff, for good reason. Also, while we shall fill out the conception, insofar as it can be done very quickly, we shall certainly not arrive at as precise a conception as might be useful in other endeavours than our own. There is no way of setting out the criteria, incidentally, which will bring together in a particular group all and only those criteria that may be seen, from all reasonable standpoints, as alike. In what follows, those that are alike from a standpoint other than mine may turn up in different groups.[4] It is also to be noted that a criterion, in the intended sense, may be more or less satisfied by an existent system of government, or, we may say, not satisfied at all.

(i) *Uncoerced Choosing and Influencing.* In the practice of democracy, to begin with certain considerations relating particularly to *pre-election* periods, the politics of the electors are not forced upon them. That is to say, roughly, that their attitudes, wants, demands and choices, both interested and in a way disinterested, are of their own making. It cannot be, certainly, that in its politics the electorate is coerced by a minority of its members, that its position is like that of a man deliberately and entirely

[4] Compare, for example, Robert Dahl, *A Preface to Democratic Theory* (Chicago, 1956), p. 84.

misled or confused. The matter is one of some complication,
however, and we shall return to it.

It is also essential, essential to the freedom of electors to act
on their politics, that there is no substantial limitation in law, or
as a matter of entrenched principle, on what citizens can be
candidates for office. The overwhelming majority can put themselves forward. In addition to this, again in order to secure the
freedom of electors, there are no legal or conventionally established
obstacles to campaigning. One must add that these possibilities of
candidacy and campaigning are possibilities in more than law and
general acceptance. They are to some extent generally available
options, not privileges which can be exercised only by a minority,
perhaps by the wealthy or by a group of men, united in ideology,
who are the instruments of the wealthy.

Finally, again principally for the reason having to do with the
freedom of electors to act on their politics, there is an effective
prohibition on the coercion of candidates. The politics of candidates are not, in a certain sense, forced upon them.

To come now to *elections*, they are regular in democracies, and
the electors make choices which are not coerced. The latter is
partly secured through the institution of free voting: electors are
able to register, can come to vote without apprehension, and, since
we are not yet in John Stuart Mill's better world, can vote
secretly. Their choices, one may add, are made in a tolerably
rational fashion. They do not individuate candidates without
reference to the politics of candidates, merely engaging in habitual
responses of a kind suggested in certain 'realist' theories of political behaviour.

After an election the government is encouraged or restrained,
but hardly controlled, not only by the evidence of the past
election but also by the continuing articulation, by rising candidates and others, of popular attitudes and responses. These have
an effect, partly, because they are indications of possible outcomes of the next election. Again there is the requirement that
the electorate is not coerced. Its attitudes and responses are not
forced upon it.

All of these features of the democratic practice, having to do
with the politics of the electorate, candidacy and campaigning,
with electoral choice, and with the exercise of influence after an
election, make for what we may label as *the uncoerced choosing*

and influencing of government. The label is attached to a group of criteria and is not to be construed as a description that might be applied to systems of government that do not in some degree satisfy the criteria. By the criteria as intended, our conception of democracy excludes the principal Communist states, whatever their virtues, and also certain conceivable states which as yet are a matter of hopeful or fearful speculation.

(ii) *Approximate Equality.* To turn now to the second group of criteria, we may recall first that democracy gives to each of almost all adults the possibility of *one* vote in the choice of a government, and the possibility of some part, *not wholly out of line with the parts of others*, in the influencing of government. The second test is distressingly vague but we shall have to get along with it as stated. Here and elsewhere, this essay can be merely a précis. It is to be noticed that we do not require that each citizen can exercise *the same* influence, but only what might be called a tolerably similar one. Were we to do so, our conception would be remote from actual political systems, and inapposite for the discussion of them. The conception, as one can conclude from the fact of its appositeness, is also a relatively ordinary one, and hence has other advantages that typically go with ordinary conceptions.

In democracy, further, as might have been left implicit in what has been said, a system obtains whereby numbers of votes issue in an affinitive government: that is, an affinitive representative or number of representatives. The term 'affinitive representation' is preferable to what is more usual, 'proportionate representation.' It is a familiar fact that in our actual political systems a party may legitimately take power despite the fact that it has got less of the popular vote than an opposing party. There are other and more common facts of what can only be called *disproportion*. Things are different in the case of complete systems of Proportional Representation. In order to avoid a conception remote from actuality, let us speak of affinitive representation. Representation is affinitive, we may cursorily say, if it results from a procedure which gives to each vote an approximately equal weight.

We need not speak of a system of influence, a system for giving effect to popular attitudes between elections, that would be a counterpart of the system just mentioned for translating votes into representation. We can perhaps imagine possibilities in this area that would lead us to attempt to specify a safeguarding criterion.

We may bring together the criteria we have, pertaining mainly to 'one man, one vote', to the derivation of representation from votes, and to a similar influence on government of the wants and opinions of individuals between elections, under the label of *approximate equality of opportunity in the choosing and influencing of government*. The criteria have the consequence, which might once have affronted a cultural piety, that the Greek *polis* was not a democracy because of the exclusion of slaves and women from the franchise. There is also the obvious and satisfactory consequence that Rhodesia and South Africa are non-democratic states.

(iii) *Effective Majority Decision*. To come to criteria of the third group, the first of them requires that elected representatives take decisions of government as a result of majority vote. Hence there are many procedures of importance having to do with the business of elected assemblies and changes in government. It is of importance, secondly, that governmental decisions, like the politics and actions of candidates and electors, are not coerced. Minorities in the society do not force decisions upon government. To use a familiar analogy, and in anticipation of reflections about coercion to which we shall come, the government does not have a gun at its head.

It is to be noticed that satisfaction of the first condition obviously allows the possibility that there exists in society a 'permanent' minority. That is, there may be a group in society, united by race, religion or politics, whose representatives have no significant possibility of entering into coalition and hence majority. The condition may also be satisfied despite the existence of certain constitutional restraints on the majority. What are excluded by the requirement in question are certain powers of veto, effective control by non-elective upper houses, and so on.

Thirdly, we require of democracy that the decisions of representatives be translated into fact. A system may be a lesser approximation of democracy because of obstruction on the part of a bureaucracy or the courts. Again, a system may fail to be democratic, or fully democratic, because to some extent the rule of law does not prevail. The requirement of rule of law may be pitched so high that all the most likely political systems would, at certain times, fail to qualify as democracies. The requirement may also be pitched so low that something close to anarchy, in a true sense of that wildly abused word, would qualify. I intend to exclude both of these possibilities.

Our third group of criteria, about the procedures of elected assemblies and the efficacy of their decisions, may be labelled as criteria having to do with *effective majority decision by government.*

This, then, is an impression, if not much more than that, of the practice I shall have in mind in speaking of democracy. The conception in question, which will be clarified in some respects in the discussion that follows, is of use in discussing such systems of government as those in Britain and America. It is not, as I have said, utopian, a conception of an *ideal democracy*, but neither is it a conception that is fully satisfied in Britain or America or like societies. Certainly it does not describe the best conceivable practice of government. Some may consider that its full realization, or the full realization of a similar but higher conception of democracy, is the best we can hope for in actual political systems.

2. VIOLENCE

Let us now spend some time, although not much, on the definition of violence and in particular of political violence. The question of definition, or what is too loosely called that, has been the subject of considerable controversy, more than it is worth. In part, the controversy has been concerned with the kind of difficulties that beset any attempt to provide an analytical definition. That is, there have been the problems that arise in any attempt to capture, with respect to something, the definition of it which is implicit in ordinary usage and belief.[5] For example, should the

[5] See, for example, the essays by Robert Audi, Robert L. Holmes, and Ronald S. Miller, in *Violence,* ed. Jerome A. Shaffer (New York, 1971).

definition of violence be so couched as to capture certain acts of speech?

In a second part, the controversy has had to do with attempts to press a definition wider than those that stand in some tolerable relation to ordinary usage and belief. We have been told that policemen, landlords, employers, shopkeepers, and indeed whole social classes and the state itself, engage in violence as a matter of course.[6] The fundamental suggestion, which has a considerable history, is not that policemen use more than the force allowed by their legal powers, that landlords send round thugs, or that the state engages in war and will use its army against revolution. Rather, it is that policemen, landlords and the state, in what most people regard as their peaceful conduct, are engaging in violence. This dispute is not essentially factual in character. We are given definitions issuing from political intention and required for simple *tu quoque* argument. Such definitions enable the man who sets a bomb to reply to those who condemn him that they, too, engage in violence, perhaps the 'violence' which others of us might describe as unfairness, victimization, or degradation.

In a third part, the so-called definitional controversy has to do with more idosyncratic suggestions. It has been suggested, as we have seen,[7] that the 'distinctively political concept of violence' is to be eschewed because it is incoherent. It is so because of its connection with the notion of what a government or a state cannot morally have, a certain right to obedience. Again, the dispute is not essentially factual. The point stands, certainly, despite complications in the distinction between the factual and the evaluative.

Whatever sympathies one may have with the political intentions implicit in the second and third parts of the controversy, one may decline to take up the recommended usage or to be bound by the intended prohibition. If one sets out only to find a clear and unimpeding definition of violence, one which does not allow

---

[6] Marcuse, in an article in the *New York Times Magazine*, 27 October, 1968, associates himself with this view. See also John Harris, 'The Marxist Conception of Violence', *Philosophy & Public Affairs*, 1974.

[7] See above, Essay 2, Parts 1–3.

spurious victories to either Left or Right, there is relatively little difficulty.

An *act of violence*, we may briefly say, is a use of considerable or destroying force against people or things, a use of force that offends against a norm. This is not to presuppose, obviously, that in one's final verdict an act of violence must be wrong. There is not much to choose between this definition and several taken by philosophers from such good sources as the *Oxford English Dictionary*. There, an act of violence is one of physical force, inflicting injury or damage on persons or property. There is something to be said for our first definition, nonetheless. Its factual and evaluative parts are marked off, and it ranges across more acts than those of injury and damage. There would be, in other enterprises than our own, a need to give attention to the notion of a norm. Let us simply substitute 'law', in the sense of criminal law, for 'norm'. Also, we may add something else, since we are not concerned with merely criminal activity but with fire raisers, bomb setters, assailants and killers whose actions are of a political kind.

Let us then, as earlier in this book,[8] define *political violence* as *a considerable or destroying use of force against persons or things, a use of force prohibited by law and directed to a change in the policies, personnel or system of government, and hence to changes in society.* The definition covers such things as race riots in America, the destruction by fire and bomb of pubs and shops in Ulster, and, in both places and also in England, the injuring, maiming and killing of citizens, policemen or soldiers. It also encompasses revolutionary violence of the past. In specifying that the uses of force be directed to certain changes in policy or government, it does not require that the agents of violence have in view highly specific aims of change. Riots may count as political violence despite the absence of well-articulated intentions of the given kind and also despite their non-rational momentum.

3. PRACTICE AND RULES

The first of the two questions raised at the beginning of this essay was that of how violence is related to the practice of democracy. That is, can one have a political system that can be said

[8] pp. 8–9.

to satisfy the conception of democracy in some reasonable degree even though political violence occurs in the given society? The question depends for its sense, obviously, on the *level* of violence that is presupposed. The latter, in good part, is a matter of numbers of injuries and deaths, amount of damage and destruction. Let us have in mind only political violence at about the level of the violence in America and Britain over the past decade. Our question, although still large, is not a difficult one. It will nonetheless be advantageous in several ways, as I shall explain, to have a tolerably clear answer. In effect, what we shall come to have will be answers to a number of smaller questions. They will be more useful than any summation.

To find our smaller questions, let us look to the criteria of democracy, beginning with the first group, those pertaining to *the uncoerced choosing and influencing of government*. Violence need not stand in the way of candidacy and campaigning, regular elections, and free voting. Violence, although it has brought appalling personal tragedy, does not in general impede or prevent these things. What of the requirements that electors and candidates are not coerced? The requirements about coercion remain unclear and more will be said of them. However, it seems evident enough that they must be so defined that violence is excluded. In a situation where violence has forms of popular support, as it commonly does, it may certainly influence, direct or suborn electors. It must be regarded as conflicting with the criterion of democracy that electors are not coerced. It must also be granted that violence conflicts with the criterion pertaining to the non-coercion of candidates. We may conclude that violence at a certain level stands in the way of a system's greater satisfaction of the given criteria of democracy.

Consider now the requirements having to do with *approximate equality of opportunity in the choosing and influencing of government*. We may put aside, as not in conflict with violence, the requirement that numbers of votes produce affinitive representation. One of the other two requirements in this group is that each citizen has one vote. If we look at this with an eye like the lens of a camera, it seems clear enough that violence is not in conflict with it. That is, violence is not generally a substantial impediment to each man's putting his ballot paper in the box or using the voting machine. To put this matter aside for a moment, there is the third criterion, to the effect that there is for each citizen a decently similar possibility of influencing the government, where that is principally a matter of giving evidence of political attitudes and inclinations. It seems true, or at any rate arguable, that political violence stands in the way of the adequate realization of this possibility. The possibility, looked at realistically, depends not only on such things as money for lobbying but also on the capability, preparedness and willingness of individuals to engage in certain lines of conduct. If a majority are in fact prevented, even if self-prevented, from engaging in acts of violence, then their possibility of influence is different from, and too much less than, that of a minority. Here, too, there is more to be said.

Let us look again at 'one man, one vote'. What is secured by this requirement? It is that each citizen has an equal role in that procedure, an election, which in a society without political violence has a certain large importance for governmental decisions. Equal roles in the procedure recommend themselves because of the effectiveness of the procedure. The criterion of democracy that each citizen has one vote is important only because we assume something about the efficacy of the election. It is not unreasonable to conclude, perhaps, that a certain level of violence in a society, since it somewhat reduces the relative efficacy of voting, is in some conflict with the criterion of 'one man, one vote'. I do not mean to suggest that in recent experience the efficacy of elections has been much reduced.

Finally, there is the third group of criteria, having to do with *effective majority decision by government*. Political violence does not conflict with the first in this group, that representative assemblies take decisions by majority vote. As for the second, that governmental decisions are not coerced, political violence clearly does stand in the way of its fuller satisfaction. The last criterion of the group is that governmental decisions are effective, and hence that the rule of law prevails. Here, it is even more difficult to judge precisely. The principal difficulty is that of setting an upper limit on violence, beyond which violence is in substantial conflict with democracy. What can be said with assurance, but not very usefully, is that any system is less democratic in the given respect if there is such an incidence of violence as that one with which we have become familiar in the past decade.

So much for one approach to our questions. Another must be made if we are to reach anything like a judicious view of how violence affects democracy. Other things also impede a fuller realization of the practice. We must be aware of them, and take them into account in a comparative view of the effect of violence. In this connection, it is clear enough that some uses of economic power ensure that systems of democracy only partially satisfy the criteria of democracy. Democracy has long been distinguished from plutocracy, in its several guises, and rightly so.

There can be no doubt that wealth, in itself and through its concomitants, makes for a coercion of electorate and candidates in their politics. The ways of this coercion are various and often covert. Constraining ideology, to mention only that, is a feature not only of alien systems. Secondly, it is clear enough that political uses of the power wielded by wealth prevent a fuller realization of the criteria having to do with equality of opportunity in the choosing and influencing of government. Dahl observed, of but one aspect of the American system, that 'if it could be quantified I suppose that Mr Henry Luce has a thousand or ten thousand times greater control over the alternatives scheduled for debate and tentative decision at a national election than I do.'[9] Thirdly, much the same situation exists in connection with the criteria of effective majority decision. The rule of law has in effect been broken through the systematic avoidance of the intended effects of legislation. In general, it is at least arguable that in every recent decade economic power has been *greatly* more effective than violence in keeping the British and American systems from being fuller realizations of democracy.

It nonetheless remains true, however balanced one's judgement, that violence does render such systems considerably less democratic than otherwise they might be. This involves the criteria concerned with ways of affecting the politics and actions of electorates and governments, with equality of opportunity in the choosing and influencing of governments, and with the rule of law.

[9] Dahl, *A Preface to Democratic Theory*, p. 72.

My principal reason for clarifying this factual proposition, that violence does render systems less democratic, is to avoid a certain vagueness and confusion. We all believe that democracy and violence somehow conflict. It is important, however, to know exactly where they do and where they do not conflict, or always conflict, and not to confuse these places. We now have one clear conflict before us. As I shall explain later, we must not make too much of this conclusion. It would be mistaken to make it decisive in the judgement of all political violence in democratic systems.

A lesser reason for clarifying the factual proposition about the practice of democracy and violence is to establish the weakness of unreflective and extravagant claims to the effect that acts of violence themselves *destroy* democracy. In general, they do not. They do less to make systems undemocratic than do acts of economic power.

It is also unreflective, incidentally, to succumb to the generalization that political violence always poses a significant *threat* to the continuation of a democratic system of government. The supposition here is that violence, however it may conflict at some moment with this or that part of the system, always carries the significant threat of an unpredictable sequence of events ending in the destruction of the system. I shall have more to say that is relevant to this supposition. It represents, often or indeed typically, an unconsidered attempt at restraint rather than a considered judgement. Indeed, the generalization that violence always threatens the existence of a democratic system is at about the level of clarity and credibility of the generalization that a democratic system always threatens its own existence. Collapses of democratic systems have as often been brought about by their own passivities as by political violence.

The first question raised at the beginning of this essay also concerns the rules of democracy. How does political violence stand in relation to them? We can deal with the matter quickly, partly for the reason that we already have the rules of democracy before us. They have emerged in the description of the democratic practice, since the most economical way of describing it is principally by way of its rules. Also, the question of violence and the rules of democracy is in a way more tractable than that of violence and systems of democracy. Many of the rules of democracy, as we have conceived it, are not determinate. Still, it is easier to conclude that behaviour counts as in infraction of a rule than to decide, as a result of certain behaviour, how far one must qualify a general description of a system which is a complex structure of rules and indeed more than that.

Guided by our findings about political violence and systems, we can conclude about political violence that it breaks the rule of democracy that electors and candidates are not to be coerced, and also the rule that each citizen is to have one vote, where that is understood to require equal participation in a fundamental procedure which gives rise to political decisions. Violence may be said to break the latter rule because the relative efficacy of the procedure is reduced. Thirdly, violence may be said to break the rule of democracy that each citizen is to have an approximately equal role in the influencing of governments, where what is in question is something other than voting. Fourthly, violence breaks the rule of democracy that governmental decisions are to be taken as binding, that the rule of law is to prevail.

We thus have a second clear conflict between violence and democracy. Violence breaks rules of the practice. This is unaffected by another fact, whatever else may be thought of it, and however it may enter into different arguments, that non-violent infractions of the rules of democracy have been more substantial than violent infractions. Non-violent infractions deriving from wealth and from class ascendancies have been more numerous and effective than violent infractions. It is worth remarking, too, that acts of violence break rules of which there is in fact some observance. It is not as if they 'broke' rulese that have been *destroyed* by infractions deriving from economic power, or rules that can be said to have always been circumvented by oppressing classes, as the Left sometimes supposes.

As in the case of the first conflict, our conclusion here must not be taken for too much. It is clear that there is no direct and unquestionable passage from the premise of something's being against a rule to the conclusion that it is wrong. That is a part of what we must now consider.

H

4. ARGUMENTS AND ENDS

The rules of democracy are no more than rules, and they do not give one what they imperfectly imply, the arguments for democracy. If one wants to know what is to be said for democracy, and how that is related to other things, one must look elsewhere than the rules. In part they are no more than means for securing ends which are cited in the arguments. The situation is familiar. If one wants to know what is to be said for keeping one's promise, one does not find it, except inchoately, in the rules of promising. The over-all rule that one must do as one promises does not give a justification for doing as one promises.

The arguments for democracy are sometimes collected into a disorder. Here we are offered the virtues of the democratic personality, there the efficiency of free-enterprise economies, here governmental stability and there the progress of science. Better can be done, I think, and without the distortion that sometimes results from a kind of reductionism. There appear to be two fundamental grounds for commitment to the practice and rules of democracy. They are a large part of the grounds of moral commitment generally.

Arguments from both these grounds have to do with the democratic practice itself and also with consequences of the practice, whether or not they are also consequences of other practices. It is no doubt a mistake to attempt to *define* the democratic practice by means of the rights, policies, customs and benefits of other kinds that generally go with it but are logically distinct from it. But, although such things are connected with the practice only contingently, they do enter into its justification. If democracies invariably, or even very often, went along with continual economic failure or a denial of non-political rights, we would have very much less to say for democracies.

One principal argument for democracy is that, compared to other practices, it gives less autonomy to any individual or minority in determining the policies of a society. Most importantly, it gives less to that minority which is made up of the governing representatives. To accept this, we need not depend on such supports as Plato's taxonomy of political systems, but on the evident nature of contemporary alternatives to democracy. We may, as a consequence of reasonable argument concerning such things as 'intraparty democracy' in the Soviet Union, be made to hesitate. We may be made to hesitate, too, by those many accusations, including the Marxist one, concerning privileged classes and minorities in our democracies. Indeed, we must amend a great deal of received doctrine. But it remains clear enough that the practice of democracy gives less autonomy to any individual or minority than do alternative forms of government.

It is to be noticed that democracy is *not* being recommended as denying the mentioned autonomy to an individual or a minority *and* giving it to ordinary people who make up the society. Such a claim is patently at odds with the facts. Democracy gives to citizens only something which can best be described briefly in a negative way: a circumstance in which no individual or minority has as much autonomy, with respect to major policies of the society, as have individuals or minorities in other political practices. It gives to citizens not any freedom *of* power but rather a freedom *from* power. The practice does this as a consequence of certain of its features enumerated at the beginning of this essay. I shall not attempt to relate this general contention, about the general absence of an autonomy in major policies, to many related praisings of democracy, some of which are wonderfully inflated.

We have so far considered only a possible autonomy which is a power to determine the policies of a society. In a democracy, no individual or minority has it. It is unreal to suppose that 'the people' have it either, although I have not said enough about the point. There are, however, other possible autonomies which in fact are realized in a democracy, or realized to some extent. These are smaller and yet enter importantly into the present fundamental argument for democracy. The argument has to do with the satisfaction and the distress of individuals, in considerable part the satisfaction of freedom and the distress of a want of it.

Some of these autonomies are integral to the practice, as defined, and are secured by what are known as the political rights. How a man will vote *is* within his decision, and his satisfaction in its being so is real. Others of these smaller autonomies are consequences rather than integral parts of the democratic practice, although not invariably so, and are in part secured by non-political rights. Here we have freedoms of culture, including religion, and freedom in the use of law. Also among the consequences of democracy are certain individual possibilities for the possession and use of natural and produced goods, both material and otherwise. This recommendation, having to do with a kind of production, is not one that is peculiar to democracy, as some of our economists have so long suggested. It seems a probability that the Soviet Union will come to have something very like it, and as probable that its not having had it in the past cannot be quickly explained by the non-democratic nature of its political system. Still, the existence of these possibilities for the possession and use of goods *is* a fact about democratic societies and hence a recommendation of them.

One fundamental argument for democracy, then, is that it secures to citizens a freedom from a certain possible power, and also secures or allows to them an array of lesser freedoms. They exercise small powers and realize certain possibilities of possession and use. This we may call *the argument of freedom*. It is related to the other fundamental ground of support for democracy, but the two are logically distinct in important ways.

One can advance the argument of freedom, correctly, on behalf of a society disfigured by extreme differences in individual powers and possibilities. Necessarily, if the argument can be used reasonably, the society is not any form of tyranny. That is, its major policies are not within the decision of an individual ruler or a minority of rulers. Nonetheless, there is no difficulty about supposing that the society in question, while it can be said to accord the lesser possibilities and powers to all, in fact distributes them in a grossly unequal way. Obviously enough, a man may truly be said to have freedoms without its being true, by some comparative test, that he has enough of them. There are situations where for two men to have a certain freedom, it must be that each has as much as the other. This is not generally so, and it is not so in the case of freedoms of the kind we are considering.

The second argument for democracy, as may be anticipated, is *the argument of equality*. It is that in a democracy one gets certain approximations to equality. Some of them are greater approximations than in non-democratic societies, others are lesser approximations. These approaches to equality, full realizations of equality in several instances, are to be found in the democratic practice itself and also in its customary consequences.

With respect to the practice, is *is* a necessary truth that if no individual or minority has autonomy with respect to the society's policies, then all have equal freedom from such autonomy. In this case, evidently, there does exist a logical connection between a freedom and its equal distribution. Even here, for good reason, we may distinguish between freedom and an equal sharing in it.

In the case of lesser freedoms which are also integral to the democratic practice, there is a closer approximation to equality than in the case of whatever analogous freedoms exist in alternative practices. In this case, the equalities in question are not entailed by the very existence of the freedoms. About this and other comparisons with alternative practices of government, incidentally, it is worth remarking that there is good reason to concentrate on those practices that have been realized and whose nature is known. There is good reason for the common reluctance to give as much attention to those alternatives which as yet are no more than objects of speculation.

The argument of equality, as noted, also concerns those freedoms which are not integral to the practice of democracy. Some of them are more equally distributed in non-democratic than in democratic societies. I have in mind approximations to economic and social equality, and all that goes with those approximations. This is a large fact, and indeed it provides an argument against democratic societies which cannot be much diminished. It is nevertheless not an argument which carries the day. No single argument can. In the case of certain other freedoms not integral to democracy, freedoms of culture and law, it does better than its alternatives.

These, then, are the two fundamental arguments for the practice of democracy. We shall have to leave unconsidered what appears to be the virtue of taking freedom and equality as the grounds of democracy rather than beginning from a premise of justice.[10] We shall also leave untouched, as I have already implied, the relationship of the two arguments to a number of derivative defences of democracy.[11]

[10] As, of course, does Rawls.
[11] All or most of them are given by Henry B. Mayo, *An Introduction to Democratic Theory* (New York, 1960).

The second question raised at the beginning of this essay was that of how political violence stands to the arguments for democracy. More particularly, how do the *ends* presupposed in these arguments stand in relation to political violence? We may approach the question by remembering that while democratic systems do make for some realization of the specified ends, they do not always do so. Historically speaking, democratic systems have not always advanced progress toward the ends of freedom and equality. They have sometimes impeded that progress. This has had to do, in part, with permanent minorities, non-accredited groups in pluralist systems, and the failure of democratic governments to respond to the intensity of distress, as distinct from its extent. It is an obvious fact that democracy has not always served progress toward the ends for Blacks in America and Catholics in the province of Ulster. This has been a question of some of the forms of freedom and some of the forms of equality. Also, of course, considerable impediments to progress have been raised up by undemocratic means.

I do not mean to suggest, however, that democratic systems have failed only in certain very isolated instances to serve the ends of freedom and equality. If one turns one's attention away from political and civil rights and the like, and thinks of the distribution of material goods and the consequences of that distribution, one encounters a larger fact. It is, as implied already, that the whole of the record of democratic systems is distressing.

There inevitably is the proposition, then, that precisely the fundamental arguments for the practice of democracy can also be used to support departures from it. The ends which are thought to be served by the rules of democracy are at least sometimes served by the breaking of the rules. This is as plain as the fact that one sometimes serves the ultimate ends of making a promise by *not* doing what one has promised to do. There is a further point. It can be argued that in some cases the *only* infractions which do effectively serve the ends of democracy are acts of political violence. The argument is in part that nothing else will work, or that nothing else will work in a reasonable time. A morally insupportable distance between privilege and deprivation will not be appreciably reduced in one lifetime, or two, by a commitment to only certain ways of affecting electorates, to 'one man, one vote', to an approximate equality in the influencing of government, and to the rule of law.

Should anyone think, incidentally, that the argument of equality must forever issue in a commitment to these things, for the reason that they constitute or approach to being equalities themselves, he needs but reflect. For example, the end specified by the argument is *equality* in its various forms, and not the equal treatment of unequals. The rule of 'one man, one unit of medical care' is a decent one if all men are similarly unhealthy. It is an indecent one when some are healthy and some are unhealthy. The rules of democracy specifying political equalities would be ideal, and not capable only of a defence *in general*, if it were the case that various freedoms, powers, and possibilities of use and possession of goods were already shared in something closer to an equal way.

I leave out, in all of this, and it is a lot left out, the claims of individuals who are members not of the societies on which we are fixing attention, our own societies, but of other societies. If the ends of the fundamental arguments for democracy can enter into a consideration of violence which has to do with the deprivation of members of our own societies, these ends can also enter into a consideration of violence which has to do with aggression against individuals in other societies.

5. DEMOCRATIC VIOLENCE

It could not be the intention of any sane person to suggest a general justification of political violence. It would be as irrational to do so as to offer a general justification of all uses of force by the state, against its own subjects or others. I do not contemplate, either, any general acceptance of the political violence of the Left. What seems to me true, although beyond being shown here, is that there is a justification of some political violence. There is, most relevantly, a moral justification for *some but not all* of what I shall call *democratic violence*. Any violence so named is to be understood as having certain characteristics, and these will play a large part in any justification it may have.

One of these features has just been given. It can be said for some political violence that it serves the ends of freedom, or equality, or both. One may argue for, although not necessarily justify, such violence as serving the ends which are also the ends of the practice of democracy, a practice which by definition is non-violent. Thus the fundamental arguments for the practice of democracy may also be used in defence of some political violence. Other types of violence, including almost all violence of the Right, cannot call upon these arguments. The proposition that violence does as a matter of fact promote progress toward freedom and equality in some circumstances can hardly be questioned. The nostrum that nothing is gained by violence does not survive a moment's reflection. It is remarkable, despite its service to entrenched interests, and to the *amour propre of* democratic politicians, that it persists at all.

The fact about ends is a considerable one, partly because the ends in question are not external to the democratic practice but internal to it. They inform the practice and are fundamental to its character. Furthermore, although the question is a large one, it may be argued that it is *uniquely* the democratic practice that is effectively directed toward both these ends. It is not as if some violence were directed toward ends of democracy, but ends not of its nature, or directed to ends of democracy clearly shared with other practices of government.

Nonetheless, we have in the fact about ends only one characteristic of democratic violence. We have, as well, only a necessary condition of the reasonableness of naming some violence as democratic. The argument does not depend on nomenclature, but if no more could be said, there would be justice in the reply that once again a term of honour was being misappropriated. More can be said.

A part of it has to do with a notion which has so far been used in this essay but hardly examined. We have seen that the democratic practice, in several ways, excludes *coercion*. A part of what is excluded, as we have granted, is violence. Let us put this aside for a moment and consider a general and fundamental separation of kinds of coercion. These may be called the coercion of force and the coercion of persuasion.

The *coercion of force* is exemplified by (i) my remaining in a room because I am bound and gagged, (ii) my giving up my wallet in the street at the point of a gun, and (iii) my injuring a man rather than allowing a number of men to be tortured or to die. In the first case talk of my *acting*, of my *doing* anything, is out of place, but the case is relevant to our concerns nonetheless. It is true in an important way, in all three cases, although for different reasons, that I am not left room for effectual reflection and judgement about what I do. This is so in the first case because only one thing, not even an action, is physically possible. It is true in the second case because only one action is possible, given a limit on human capability which we all accept. I could try to keep my wallet, but only at a risk which I am not expected to take. I am left no room for effectual judgement in the third case either. Only one action is possible, at least if the situation is not complicated in certain ways, given a moral prohibition which has quite general acceptance.

It is evident enough that these three cases differ in a certain respect. The first involves a single physical possibility, the second a single human possibility, and the third a single moral possibility. They are alike in that they offer but a *single* possibility and hence that there is no room for effectual reflection and judgement. As a consequence of this, although the fact is of secondary importance to us, I am absolved from a certain responsibility in each case. I may be responsible for an act which gave rise to any of the situations, but that is irrelevant. The third case raises various questions, but it is surely true, in an important sense, that I would not be held responsible for injuring the man.

The *coercion of persuasion* can be illustrated by my giving an unwilling donation to a dubious charity when I believe that the collector will mention a refusal to my employer, who is in favour of the charity. Another example of the coercion of persuasion is my not intervening in a man's denigrating talk about my friend since I believe the man has just been badly upset by a personal affront. I am restrained, not willingly, by my belief about his state of mind. My restraint may or may not appear to me to have a moral ground. In both cases, I am left room for effectual reflection and judgement.

I do not wish to assert that there is a distinction of a certain kind between the coercion of force and the coercion of persuasion. That is, I do not wish to assert that there is a criterion such that all instances of coercion fall clearly into one category or the other. It would be surprising if this were true. Many instances *do* fall into one category or the other, and this is sufficient for my argument. I do not suppose either, of course, that the two coercions have been fully analysed or all questions about them answered.

To return to the relevant criteria of democracy, it is evident that they require that the electorate as a whole not be subject to the coercion of force. If an electorate is subject to the coercion of force, the system of government in question is necessarily a tyranny. It is, indeed, principally because of the obvious need to distinguish democracy from tyranny that the criteria of democracy pertaining to coercion appear to be, as they are, unquestionable.

However, are the criteria to be understood in such a way that the electorate in a democracy cannot be subject to the coercion of persuasion, in any form? If they are so understood, then no existing system of government is within sight of satisfying the criteria and none ever has been. The practice of democracy is such that it is possible for minorities and interest groups to exert pressure on the electorate. These pressures sometimes stand in analogy with those persuasions of individuals mentioned above. They sometimes evoke moral responses and sometimes evoke responses of prudence, but not what we may call enforced prudence. It is hardly too much to say that the democratic practice has at its bottom the coercion of persuasion. The electorate is restrained or constrained, but in such a way that it is left room for reflection. The same is true for candidates and governments.

It may be supposed, at this point, that violence conflicts with democracy, as we have seen it does, because it consists, always, in the coercion of force. It does not. Some violence consists in the coercion of persuasion. Governments, to speak first of them, are left room for effectual reflection and decision in the face of this violence. The American government was not *forced*, by acts of violence, to enter into a more vigourous policy against racial discrimination and racism. It was certainly not *forced* by violence, although the point takes us out of the area of our primary concern, to change its policy of war in Vietnam. The British government was not *forced* to take seriously the demands of the oppressed minority in Ulster. A man whose shop is destroyed by a fire or a bomb, or a man who abandons his shop in the face of the direct threat of fire or bomb, *is* subjected to the coercion of force. Such facts, and also the facts of injury and death, must enter into reflection and count against violence. It remains true that governments are not subjected to the coercion of force by such acts. The case is similar with electorates and with candidates. With few exceptions, they are not forced into their politics by violence or forced into particular political behaviour.

We have it, then, that while violence is excluded by the criteria of democracy having to do with coercion, it cannot be that these criteria exclude the coercion of persuasion. It follows, then, that violence is not excluded as being coercion of persuasion. The exact ground is different. To come to the principal point, some violence shares an attribute with procedures allowed by the criteria of democracy, procedures which are basic to democratic systems. Some violence is a matter of the coercion of persuasion. It is fundamentally different from behaviour which leaves no option to electorates, candidates and governments. The second feature of democratic violence, then, is just this, that it consists only in the coercion of persuasion and so shares an attribute with activity that is integral to the democratic practice.[12]

The third characteristic of democratic violence has to do with equality. It was granted above that political violence conflicts with the criteria of democratic practice which require an approximation to equality of influence for all citizens. Violence may give to individuals who engage in it a greater degree of influence than is enjoyed by some of the majority of individuals who do not engage in it. It was granted, too, that violence breaks other equality-rules of the democratic practice. Still, there is another

---

[12] Rawls (*A Theory of Justice*, p. 366 and elsewhere) suggests that violence cannot be a 'mode of address', a form of notice given to a society that injustice exists. If it is true that violence cannot be described as a 'mode of address', it is also true that typically it does not consist in the coercion of force. My argument depends in part on this latter point rather than any doubtful suggestion about a close connection between violence and more formal or venerable proceedings. In my view, as may be anticipated, violence may on occasion be described as 'an appeal to the sense of justice of the majority', which Rawls appears to deny.

consideration. Of the individuals who do not engage in violence, as we have noticed, there are some who enjoy very great favourable inequalities of influence. That is, wealth and position give to some considerable number of individuals a far greater influence than is had by almost all of those individuals who are without wealth or position. Let us compare, then, the group of the violent and the group of the privileged. It is plain enough that the violent may be seen as attempting to secure an equal influence or something like it. For the most part, they do not succeed.

It must be admitted that the violent are securing or attempting to secure a favourable inequality when compared with a majority of the citizens of their society. This proposition is a ground for our conclusions concerning criteria and rules. The proposition will be of importance, too, in any final assessment of violence. At the same time, it is entirely relevant that violence by another comparison may be an attempt to secure *equality* of influence, or an approximation of it. All of this, needless to say, is of a schematic character and calls out for improvement of several kinds. The result of a more extended examination, I suggest, will be a conclusion of the kind we have. It is that some violence has an affinity with a feature of the democratic practice. A criterion of that practice is that there is an approximation of equality of influence. Some violence, by one important comparison, is an attempt to approximate more closely to an equality of influence.

A fourth characteristic of democratic violence is that it is *not* directed to the destruction of a democratic system. This is true of most of the violence with which we are familiar. It is not revolutionary in reality, whatever the accompanying rhetoric. That is, it does not have as its object the establishment of a radically different system, one that is non-democratic. In this respect, it is similar to almost all civil disobedience. To suppose that all violence is revolutionary, and that all violence in democratic systems is aimed at the overthrow of those systems, is to fly in the face of the evidence of the present and the past.

There is also a fifth characteristic, related to the fourth. It is not merely that violence of the kind I have in mind is not directed to the destruction of democratic systems, but that its effects are likely to be that the systems in question become fuller realizations of democracy in certain respects. That this has been the consequence of violence in the historical development of a number of governmental systems is as established a fact as that democratic systems have had their beginnings in revolutionary violence.

Violence, then, may serve the ends which are fundamental to the democratic practice. Secondly, it may, as coercion share an attribute with procedures that are intrinsic to democratic systems. It cannot be said without dismay and apprehension, but it is to be said that some bombs are like votes. Thirdly, this violence is by one comparison an attempt to gain equality of influence. Fourthly, it is not directed to the ending of democratic systems. It may, finally, lead to their becoming more democratic.

6. JUSTIFICATION

To review the entire course of this essay, we began with the practice of democracy and with political violence, and passed on to a number of propositions. (i) Political violence renders the system of government of a society less democratic, as to a greater extent do certain uses of economic power. This is one conflict between democracy and violence. (ii) Political violence conflicts with certain of the rules of democracy. Although the same is true of economic power, we here have a second conflict between democracy and violence. (iii) Some violence, as we have just seen, may serve the ends given in the fundamental arguments for the practice of democracy. Here, it is mistaken to find conflict. Some of the violence in question, further, has other features of as much importance. It may be named democratic violence.

This latter part of this exercise in particular has relevance to the general question of the justification of political violence. That is, I have not pointed to similarity between the democratic practice and one kind of political violence, democratic violence, only in order to establish the fact of similarity. Rather, it has been my intention to bring into clearer view something that will make less difficult our judgement of political violence. It seems true that in considering problematic behaviour, it is a great advantage if we can see clearly its relations to unproblematic behaviour. If in personal relations a man acts in an ambiguous way, and his action requires some kind of appraisal, that appraisal will be facilitated by our seeing to what extent his action has the character of a threat, say, or a warning. It is when his action cannot be assimilated to anything which already has been the subject of reflection and judgement that there is the greatest difficulty.

Some political violence has features that are shared with the practice of democracy, and that practice has a large recommendation. These are facts of which we are morally obliged to take account. We have in them one significant bridge between facts about our societies, the facts of inequality, and substantial conclusions about political violence.

I have said that it seems to me that at least some violence has a moral justification, but I have not done anything like show this. It will be clear, I trust, that I do not suppose that the proposition that some violence has a justification can be derived from the fact alone that it is in the given sense democratic. To think violence can be justified this way is as mistaken as taking as a justification of a policy the fact by itself that the policy issues from the democratic practice. If some bombs are like votes, they also maim and kill. The deprivation and degradation that call up violence should never be absent from thought and feeling, and not so present in them as to obscure other terrible realities.

Index